eat * sleep * shop

LONDON

STYLE GUIDE

fully
revised &
updated
edition

saska graville

photography by
jessica reftel evans & martin reftel

MURDOCH BOOKS

For Dad, who loved to travel the world,
but was always happiest coming home to London.

contents

welcome to london style

I'M A LONDONER, BORN AND BRED and I love
my hometown. It has a personality and style all its own—
from grand to edgy, modern to heritage and urban to shabby
chic. London is such a vast, sprawling, living, breathing entity
that it's impossible to give it a neat and convenient label.
And that's what makes me love it all the more.

But there is, I believe, AN ESSENCE TO LONDON
STYLE, and you find it in the small, off-the-radar places: the
one-off shops, street markets, corner pubs and local restaurants
that Londoners themselves go to. These places share a certain
eccentricity, quirkiness and independence of spirit. And that's
what this book is all about.

You don't need me to tell you about the 'trophy' sites—the palaces,
museums, parks and famous shops—but I will share with you the
places that you're not going to find in an average guide book. I'll
tell you where to rummage for vintage furniture on a Saturday
morning (no, not Portobello Market, everyone knows about that
and it's priced for tourists), the tiny A-list florist you'll fall in love
with (the one Nigella Lawson swears by), the local pub beloved by
the country's fussiest food critic, and the two-bedroom B&B that
gets booked months in advance.

In other words, I'LL GET YOU UNDER THE SKIN OF
THIS INTOXICATING CITY, introducing you to the lesser-
known addresses and some of the people behind them. I make
no claims for this book as a comprehensive guide to London—I'm
assuming a certain amount of prior knowledge on your part of the
classics like Selfridges and Liberty—but it will give you the chance
to scratch the surface just a little bit more.

London is, of course, huge and even Londoners are pretty clueless about its geography when you transplant them out of their comfort zones. IT'S IMPOSSIBLE TO COVER IT ALL IN ONE GO, so don't even try. Instead, tackle it an area at a time. I've divided the city geographically into North, South, East, West and Central, and then within each area are the 'villages' that create London's personality. My advice? Pick an area, go for a wander in one village, and then get yourself an Oyster travel card (for all London travel) to zip off to another village in the same area.

Within each village, I've included a mix of the most stylish and individual places for shopping, eating, drinking and sleeping—all the important things. I'll also introduce you to some of the Londoners themselves, who I've persuaded to share their favourite local haunts. From fashion to furniture to food, I'll direct you to the spots that you won't find on the average high street. I'll give you options for breakfast, lunch, supper and everything in between. And when it comes to a bed for the night, I'll point you in the direction of some of the city's sleekest check-ins (some tiny, some a little bit grander).

Enjoy your time in my hometown. I hope that this book reveals a side to my city that you wouldn't otherwise have seen. There'll always be somewhere new to discover, and that's the joy that is London—one trip is never enough. See you again soon.

my 24-hour wishlist

Let's pretend that geography is no object. If I could plot my perfect London day from the places featured in this book, here's where I'd go...

*I'd start with breakfast at **Granger & Co** (see page 284)—no one does avocado on rye toast and a flat white as well as Bill Granger. I'd avoid the Portobello Market crowds, and go instead to nearby **Golborne Road** (see page 196), where the cluster of interiors shops sells some of the most interesting homewares in London. Then I'd head over to **Bermondsey** (see page 50) to do my food shopping from the producers who have decamped to Maltby Street and its surrounds from the (much busier) Borough Market. Lunch would be a pizza at **Story Deli** in Shoreditch (see page 163), followed by a stroll along **Columbia Road** (see page 98), buying flowers and popping into the quirky, independent shops that open only at the weekend. Shopping done, I'd head south of the river to **Olympic Studios** (see page 289) in Barnes, where I grew up, for supper in the heritage glamour of the Members' Club, followed by a film screening in the state-of-the-art cinema. Last but not least, I'd check in to **Dean Street Townhouse** in Soho (see page 272), for a night of urban luxury in one of my favourite hotels. A perfect day.*

*PS Were I a bit more adventurous, I'd book into **The Family Business** (see page 94) for a work-of-art tattoo, but I'll leave that for someone else's dream day.*

Sasha Granville

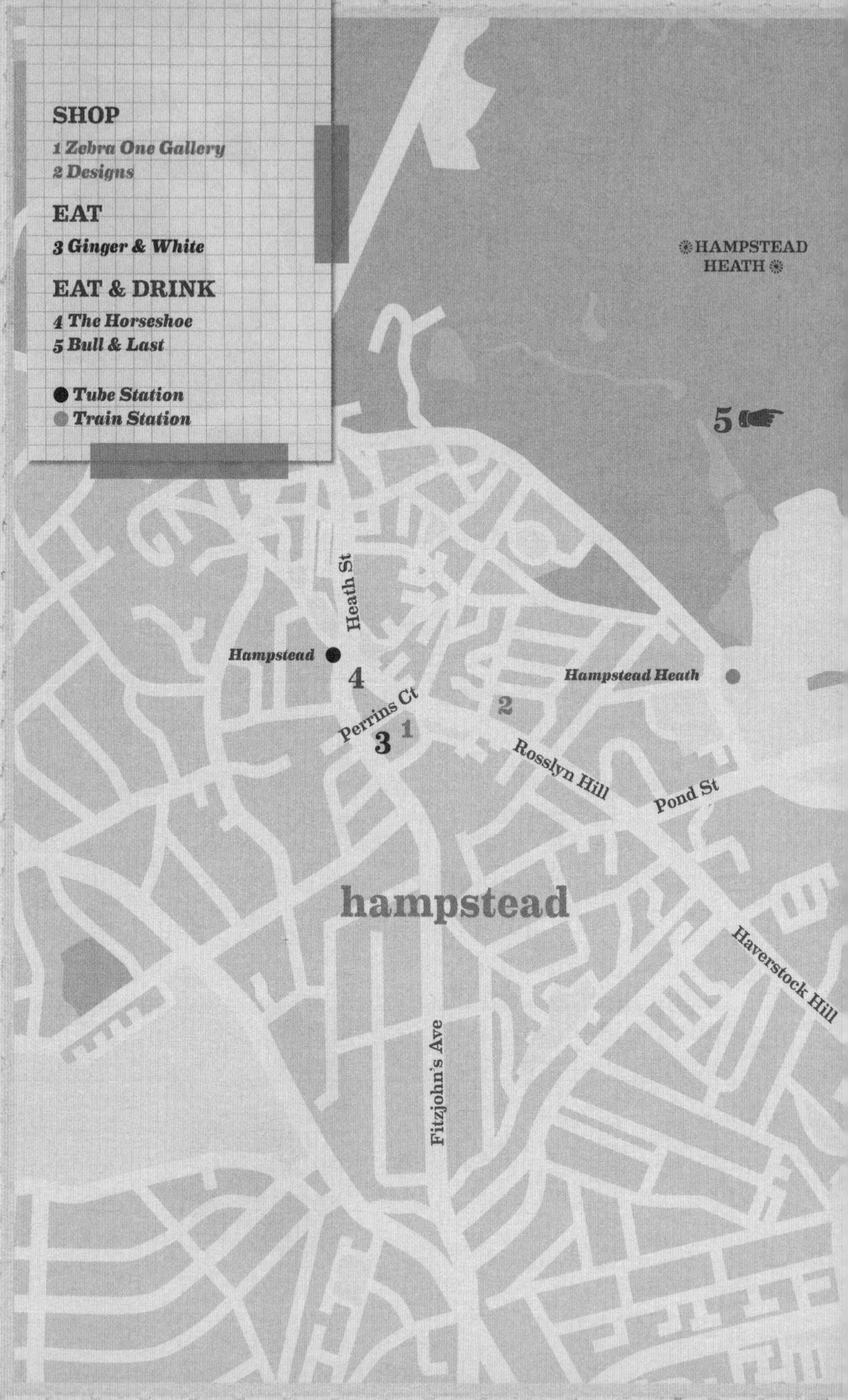
SHOP
1 Zebra One Gallery
2 Designs
EAT
3 Ginger & White
EAT & DRINK
4 The Horseshoe
5 Bull & Last
Tube Station
Train Station
HAMPSTEAD HEATH
5
Heath St
Hampstead
4
Perrins Ct
3
1
2
Hampstead Heath
Rosslyn Hill
Pond St
hampstead
Haverstock Hill
Fitzjohn's Ave

Nhampstead

Undoubtedly one of London's most beautiful areas, with the 790 acres of wild and unspoilt Hampstead Heath on its doorstep and the sort of grand residential architecture that most of us can only dream of. Shopping-wise, it tends towards chain stores and slightly twee, overpriced interiors shops, with not as many cool, independent places as you might hope for. But it's worth a visit nonetheless. Get lost on the Heath and then head to one of the area's pubs for a long lunch.

1*

2

1*

2

1* ZEBRA ONE GALLERY

You don't expect to find a pocket of rock 'n' roll glamour in a Hampstead back street, but that's exactly what owner Gabrielle du Plooy has created in her Zebra One Gallery. If iconic photography is your thing, the range of work she sells is unmissable. All of it with heavy pop culture references, all of it limited edition and signed by the artist. There's a naked Kate Moss shot by Kate Garner, Andy Warhol's iconic Marilyn, as well as Bert Stern's images from the actress's last ever shoot. David Bowie, Jimi Hendrix and Michael Caine all put in an appearance. Don't be fooled by the narrow cobbled laneway and olde-worlde wonky shop front, this is a must-visit destination for any fans of modern photography. There's also a consultancy service if you're in the market for an art-overhaul of your home. A few Marilyns and a couple of Kates? Sorted.

1 Perrins Court
NW3 1QX
0207 794 1281
www.zebraonegallery.com

2* DESIGNS

You could easily walk past this understated dress shop, and not have a clue about the miraculous bargains within. Skip it at your peril. Owner Dominique Cussen runs one of North London's busiest nearly-new designer fashion outlets. (At least one top fashion editor is not going to be happy that her secret go-to for Marni bargains is being revealed in this book.) Alexander McQueen, Dolce & Gabbana, YSL, Stella McCartney—all the huge labels are here, donated in mint condition by owners who simply fell out of love with them. A copper quilted Rochas opera coat is a snip at £185. Or a black Chanel jacket for £360? Hard to leave it there. Shoes and bags add to the temptations. No wonder Dominique has had an enthusiastic and loyal following since she opened her shop's door 30 years ago. A local institution.

60 Rosslyn Hill
NW3 1ND
Tel 0207 435 0100
www.designsnw3.co.uk

4✳ THE HORSESHOE

A gastropub with the X factor. Not only is the food great and the room lovely, but the place brews its own ales. The main room boasts big wooden tables, giant windows and cool art on the walls. So far, so *not* your average pub. And how many pubs credit the provenance of the food on the menu—St Austell Bay mussels, roast Cornish cod, and all the meat from one Suffolk butcher who uses local farms. The perfect spot for a long Sunday lunch, or just a quick drink at the bar.
28 Heath Street
NW3 6TE
0207 431 7206
www.the horseshoehampstead.com

5✳ BULL & LAST

No wonder one of the UK's most influential food critics, Giles Coren, loves this pub so much, raving about the 'best pub food' he's ever eaten. Technically in Highgate, but right on the edge of Hampstead Heath, it's everything a neighbourhood local should be: outstanding food, a great room to hang out in and some of the friendliest staff in London. Nothing to find fault with. There's even a canine menu for your four-legged friend, featuring pig's ears and roast marrow bones. Pop in for Sunday lunch and you'll find the likes of crisp pig's cheek, basil, watermelon, mint and sesame on the menu—a cut above the usual pub grub. And don't leave without trying the Scotch eggs sold at the bar—worth a visit for one of those alone. If the weather's nice, order a picnic hamper and head over the road to Hampstead Heath; not many pubs offer a service like that.
168 Highgate Road
NW5 1QS
0207 267 3641
www.thebullandlast.co.uk

tonia george, emma scott and nick scott

Search out this small enclave of pared-back urban chic amid the tweeness of the rest of Hampstead. Ginger & White owners Tonia George, Emma Scott and Nick Scott preside over a tiny, always-packed café that not only serves some of the best coffee in London, but flies the flag for Best of British. Your sausage sarnie boasts Wicks Manor sausages, free-range eggs are from Treflach Farm and the goat's cheese is Capricorn Somerset. Sit at the communal table, gazing at the Union Jack print and jar of wild English flowers, and the effect is all very Cool Britannia.

GINGER & WHITE
4a–5a Perrins Court NW3 1QS ✻ **0207 431 9098** ✻ *www.gingerandwhite.com*

> '*A melting pot of styles and flavours is what defines London*'

How would you define London style?
The only rule is that there are no rules! A melting pot of styles and flavours is what defines London.

Where do you go in London to be inspired?
The low rents in the East of London have spawned a wealth of boutiques and small businesses that seem to defy the commercial trend that was leading to the homogenisation of London high streets.

Your favourite local places?
Zebra One Gallery on Perrins Court (see page 11) sells amazing photography, and Villa Bianca (www.villabiancagroup.co.uk) is an old-school Italian restaurant still elegantly serving food in a way that feels unchanged over 30 years of business.

What's in your secret shopping address book?
La Fromagerie in Marylebone (see page 222) has an awe-inspiring cheese room and

15

Where's the best place for a weekend supper?

We love The Hawksmoor (www.thehawksmoor.com). It's all about the flavour of meat here, and although the food is very classic and unadorned, the service is friendly—no old-fashioned sycophantic 'us and them' attitude between waiting staff and diners.

Best place for a drink?

The Shop in Kensal Rise (www.theshopnw10.com) serves great cocktails in jam jars and the space is cosy and intimate—with a piano if you feel like breaking out into song.

Your favourite breakfast spot?

Obviously Ginger & White, but also **Caravan** in Kings Cross (see page 253) or the **Towpath Café** (see page 142).

Where do you go in London to relax?

In the summer the amazing stainless steel-lined lido in Parliament Hill is the best place to be. It feels like a little oasis and has a lot of charm.

Favourite cultural sights?

A visit to the Courtauld Institute of Art in Somerset House (www.courtauld.ac.uk) for a view of art that's a manageable size. And Somerset House itself (www.somersethouse.org.uk) at Christmas, for ice skating.

Top three things that every visitor to London should do?

Kew Gardens (www.kew.org) for great displays of horticulture, the biggest pumpkins at Halloween and huge greenhouses full of all kinds of plants from around the world. Leighton House Museum (www.rbkc.gov.uk/museums), a real Aladdin's cave of Victorian Arabic tiles. And the view of London from the top of Parliament Hill.

wonderful produce. You can spend a fortune in there and have lunch. Next door is the Ginger Pig (www.thegingerpig.co.uk), who do the meatiest sausage rolls which ooze and dribble down your chin.

Describe your perfect out-and-about weekend?

Breakfast on wild sourdough at **E5 Bakehouse** (see page 120), then head down Broadway Market to **Climpson & Sons** (see page 126), go down by the canal and have lunch at the **Towpath Café** (see page 142), a quirky place made out of storage arches, with food that's cooked from the heart. Head into town for some shopping at Selfridges (www.selfridges.com) and end up with a soothing bowl of udon noodles for dinner at Koya (www.koya.co.uk) in Soho.

17

SHOP

1 Fandango
2 Clarissa Hulse
3 Annie's
4 Folklore
5 Atelier Abigail Ahern

EAT & DRINK

6 The Drapers Arms
7 The Elk in the Woods
8 Ottolenghi
9 The Duke of Cambridge

● Tube Station
● Train Station

Corsica St

2

● ● Highbury & Islington

Canonbury Ln

4

Canonbury Rd

Upper St

Barnsbury St

8

Essex Road

Almeida St

Cross St

5

1

islington

Theberton St

Barnsbury Rd

Essex Rd

Packington St

Liverpool Rd

St Peter's St

7

3

9

Charlton Pl

● Angel

Pentonville Rd

City Rd

N
islington

north

There's nothing up and coming about Islington; it is well and truly up and come. Upper Street offers an endless choice of smart shops and cafés, while picturesque Camden Passage is a treasure trove of vintage and antique boutiques and market stalls. In leafy Barnsbury, you'll find streets of elegant white houses—former British Prime Minister Tony Blair was a local—and chic gastropubs. No wonder Islingtonites can't imagine living anywhere else.

20

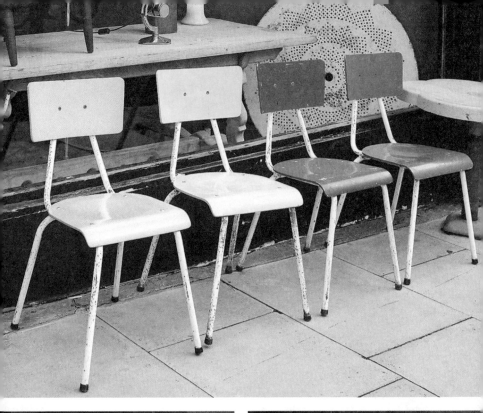

1 ✳ FANDANGO

Billed as 'sustainable luxury', this tiny
wedge-shaped store has a small but
perfectly formed selection of wares, all
of them with a glossy edge. From rare
19th-century sunburst mirrors to Murano
glass apothecary jars and sets of antlers,
everything has been beautifully restored.
This is not the place for shabby chic.
Instead, anything you pick will add a
bit of drama and glamour to your home.
A treasure trove.
2 Cross Street
N1 2BL
Tel 07979 650 805
www.fandangointeriors.co.uk

2 ✻ CLARISSA HULSE

Hidden down a residential street, this is textile designer Clarissa Hulse's first stand-alone shop, and it's glorious. With her botanically inspired prints already in huge demand by the likes of Liberty, Heal's and Selfridges, Clarissa has taken over the space in front of her design studio to showcase the full range of her wares. Colour-phobes, look away. The shop is a riot of jewel-like shades: glowing greens, hot pinks, sparkling blues. There isn't any minimal white in sight. From fabrics to cushions to scarves and even notebooks, it's a masterclass in how to style your home happy. Everything is displayed on pieces of vintage furniture: the cast-iron bed made up with the richly patterned sheets looks so seductively inviting, you'll want to move right in.

29 Corsica Street
N5 1JT
Tel 0207 226 7055
www.clarissahulse.com

23

3 ✷ ANNIE'S

When you can boast Kate Moss as a customer, you know that your stash of vintage costume and textiles is pretty much as good as it gets. This is vintage with an edge. There are no slightly smelly or scruffy goods here, just beautifully curated groupings of bygone style. Wedding dresses are a specialty (a gorgeous lace one from 1948 is £150), along with flimsily sexy slips, vintage ribbons and trimmings, fur coats, even swimsuits. Rummage the rails and the quality is quickly apparent.

12 Camden Passage
N1 8ED
Tel 0207 359 0796
www.anniesvintageclothing.co.uk

4✳ FOLKLORE

Life feels calm, ordered and neatly arranged in Folklore. With a focus on simple, quality design, the shop sells a mix of homewares and furniture, all of it with a clean, Scandi-esque aesthetic. There's no room for clutter in Folklore's world. You'll want to fill your kitchen cupboards with rows of grey enamel mugs and glass and metal storage jars, kit out your living room with monochrome-hued blankets and throws, and place elegant, grey wood chairs around your dining table. You'll even find yourself craving a cluster of perfectly sharpened pencils. Adding to the shop's charm is its heritage setting—the gold leaf signage from a previous retail incarnation is still above the door. Not very minimal Scandi, but gorgeous all the same.

193 Upper Street
N1 1RQ
Tel 0207 354 9333
www.shopfolklore.com

27

'No wonder Islingtonites can't imagine living anywhere else'

6✳ THE DRAPERS ARMS

Off the beaten track in one of Islington's
most exclusive enclaves, this is the perfect
neighbourhood pub. Forget images of a
dark, smoky boozer, this is cool and chic
from the moment you walk in. The elegant
Georgian building boasts high, stencilled
ceilings that create an open, airy feel to
the room, while white tiling and shades of
pale green on the walls add to the lightness.
Seasonal menus change daily; dishes like
whole Dorset crab with mayonnaise and
salad, and guinea fowl, bacon and prune
pie, put this in a different league to your
average pint-and-packet-of-crisps watering
hole. The annual December carol singing
night is a locals' favourite.

44 Barnsbury Street
N1 1ER
Tel 0207 619 0348
www.thedrapersarms.com

7✳ THE ELK IN THE WOODS

With a look that's all its own, this
quirky restaurant is a one-off worth
seeing. Think hunting lodge meets
antique shop. A stuffed stag's head takes
pride of place, opposite a pink wall of
vintage mirrors. Old ceramic tiling sits
alongside quirkily modern wallpaper. It's
slightly mad but it works. As for the food,
from the breakfast bacon sarnie to the
night-time small dishes of game pâté
and chorizo and pancetta stew, there's
a steady stream of treats to keep the
crowds of locals happy.

37–39 Camden Passage
N1 8EA
Tel 0207 226 3535
www.the-elk-in-the-woods.co.uk

8*

9*

8✳

8✳ OTTOLENGHI

One of four cafés in the Ottolenghi
empire, this is the biggest and the best.
Abundance doesn't quite do it justice:
the white, airy room is groaning with
trays of exquisitely delicious-looking
food. No other decoration is needed.
Plump cherries sit on mini-cheesecakes,
raspberries adorn lemon cupcakes,
passionfruit meringues show off their
perfect peaks. If you can tear your
eyes away from the sweet goodies,
the other side of the room tempts with
Mediterranean-inspired savouries like
roasted beetroot, and goat's cheese and
onion marmalade tart. Mouthwatering.
287 Upper Street
N1 2TZ
0207 288 1454
www.ottolenghi.co.uk

9✳

9✳ THE DUKE OF CAMBRIDGE

Britain's first and only Soil Association
certified gastropub is not just one
hundred per cent organic, it's also a
stylish hideaway. Tucked down a leafy
side street, if you didn't know it was
there, you'd easily miss it. With menus
that change twice daily to reflect what
the suppliers have brought in (big
multinationals and chain stores are
shunned), the food is proudly sustainable
and delicious. No wonder it's a repeated
winner of the London Dining Pub of the
Year. As for the design, the main room
has the cool factor: big wooden tables,
mismatched chairs and funky green
industrial light fittings. Definitely not
your average pub.
30 St Peter's Street
N1 8JT
Tel 0207 359 3066
www.dukeorganic.co.uk

abigail ahern

Interior designer, retailer, product designer and writer, Abigail Ahern is multi-talented and hugely influential. As an interior designer, her work has included the Ritz-Carlton's spa in Palm Beach, Florida, while her products, such as her collection of lighting, are sold in Harrods and The Conran Shop (see page 75). But it's for her own shop, Atelier Abigail Ahern, that she's mainly known and loved. An Aladdin's cave of interiors goodies, the walls are painted dark (with Abigail's beloved London Clay shade from designer paint company, Farrow & Ball), candles burn, and an abundance of buys fills every nook and cranny. Choose from classic pieces such as vases, cushions and throws, or embrace Abigail's quirky chic taste with one of her own-designed British bulldog lamps.

ATELIER ABIGAIL AHERN
137 Upper Street N1 1QP ❀ 0207 354 8181 ❀ www.abigailahern.com

'Parks inspire me, especially the Royal parks, watching the seasons change'

How would you define London style?
Edgy, experimental and innovative. I don't know whether it's because we live in such a cosmopolitan city, or whether the weather makes us want to cheer ourselves up by being as creative as possible, or a combo of both. Either way, we love to mix and match, mingle vintage with high street and modern and use some high-voltage doses of colour.

Where do you go in London to be inspired?
I walk a lot with my dog, so parks inspire me, especially the Royal parks, watching the seasons change. They constantly inspire with new interesting colour combinations. I also adore markets: Portobello, Borough and **Columbia Road** (see page 98).

Your favourite local places?
There are so many. **Violet** (see page 132) for the yummiest coffee and cakes—open the door and the most delicious smell of baking fills the air. Other local favourite places include **Broadway Market** (see page 125) every Saturday to stock up on groceries and wander around the cute stores.

Describe your perfect out-and-about weekend?

A drive to **Petersham Nurseries** (see page 280), parking in Richmond and strolling along the river to this beautiful nursery and Michelin-starred restaurant. Then an afternoon spent wandering through Hyde Park and Green Park, ending up at Gordon's Wine Bar (www.gordonswinebar.com) for a late-afternoon glass of wine. Sunday wouldn't be Sunday without a stroll to Columbia Road (see page 98) for flowers, brunch at **Brawn** (see page 113) or **Pizza East** (see page 161), a wander around Brick Lane (www.visitbricklane. org) and then home—usually via a drink at the **Cat & Mutton** (see page 130) with a big bundle of newspapers.

What's in your secret shopping address book?

For interiors, **Labour and Wait** in Redchurch Street (see page 153), **Fandango** (see page 21) in Islington for vintage and The Dog and Wardrobe (www.thedogandwardrobe.com) on Broadway Market. Then all the super-sweet vintage clothes shops in Camden Passage. Go at the weekend and a tiny-teeny market sets up there, too. Not forgetting **Nelly Duff** (see page 101) in Columbia Road for art.

Where's the best place for a weekend supper?

A Little of What You Fancy (www. alittleofwhatyoufancy.info) in a seedy bit of the Kingsland Road in Dalston, where I live. The food is fabulous and much of it comes from neighbourhood gardens—imagine organic roast rainbow trout with pink fir apple potatoes, or slow-braised oxtail with red wine, herbs and garlic. Yummy.

Best place for a drink?

The bar at Moro (www.moro.co.uk) with a spot of tapas, or the bar at **Pizza East** (see page 161) for people-watching.

Your favourite breakfast spot?

Towpath Café (see page 142) for cappuccino with granola, seasonal berries and yoghurt. They make everything from scratch. Or the **E5 Bakehouse** (see page 120) under the arches in London Fields, where they bake and sell totally amazing bread.

Where do you go in London to relax?

I walk or I swim—Hyde Park, Green Park and Victoria Park are the lungs of our city and immediately relax me the moment I enter. Also, the outdoor pool at the bottom of my road, London Field's Lido (www.hackney.gov.uk/c-londonfields-lido.htm). Nothing makes me feel better than a good swim outside.

Top three things that every visitor to London should do?

Borough Market (www.boroughmarket. org.uk) is a must to sample some of our fabulous British produce, drink coffee at Monmouth and then stroll along the river towards the Embankment. Wander around Shoreditch and Dalston—small stores, little cafés and art galleries abound. It's edgy and eclectic with a great vibe, and for me pretty much personifies what London is all about. And the London Eye (www. londoneye.com) is brilliant for a bird's-eye view of the city.

35

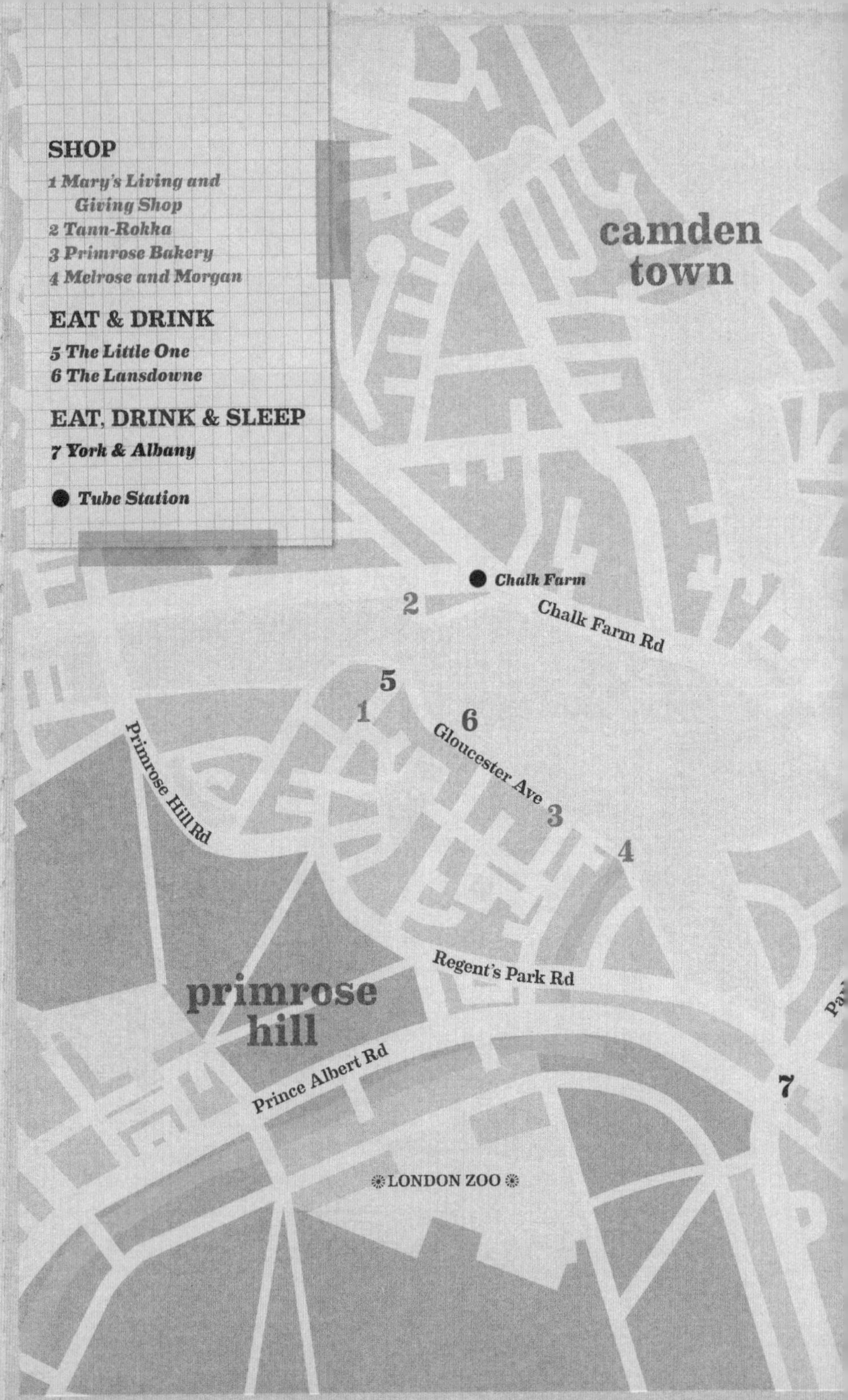
SHOP
1 Mary's Living and Giving Shop
2 Tann-Rokka
3 Primrose Bakery
4 Melrose and Morgan
EAT & DRINK
5 The Little One
6 The Lansdowne
EAT, DRINK & SLEEP
7 York & Albany
Tube Station
camden town
Chalk Farm
Chalk Farm Rd
Gloucester Ave
Primrose Hill Rd
Regent's Park Rd
primrose hill
Prince Albert Rd
LONDON ZOO
1
2
3
4
5
6
7

primrose hill

north

Primrose Hill is shorthand for 'where London's A-listers live'. Jamie Oliver and his family reside in two knocked-together houses near the park, with singers Gwen Stefani, Gavin Rossdale and their sons just down the road. Rocker Noel Gallagher has moved on, but sold his mansion to Little Britain's David Walliams, so the celeb quota is still high. With its pretty streets and proximity to Regent's Park and central London, it's easy to see why it's one of the city's best-loved spots. Come and browse the shops, then grab a coffee and hike up to the top of Primrose Hill for one of the city's most romantic views. You'll be charmed.

1✳MARY'S LIVING AND GIVING SHOP

British TV personality and retail guru Mary Portas, herself a Primrose Hill local, has reinvented the traditional image of a fusty charity shop with her own-name outlets for Save the Children. Forget any notions about crammed rails of dodgy, unwanted items. Here, the space is curated like a treasure trove of clothes, books and homeware. The back is styled like a living room, with leather armchairs, wooden bookshelves and old Turkish rugs on the floor. At the front, a chandelier hangs over the rails of donated clothes. Comedian Ricky Gervais is among the high-profile shoppers you might spot in search of a bargain.

109 Regent's Park Road
NW1 8UR
Tel 0207 586 9966
www.savethechildren.org.uk

2 ✳ TANN-ROKKA

Do not miss this hoard of antique homeware and bespoke designs, crammed into what used to be the ticket office of Primrose Hill train station. The first thing to strike you is the mass of chandeliers hung the length of the narrow room. The effect is magical. The owner has classic taste with a twist. Mirrored and more traditional pieces of furniture sit alongside deer antlers painted and studded with Swarovski crystals—a favourite with the local A-listers. When you've had your fill, cross the street and see if the shop's tea garden is open; its hours are seasonal and weekends only. With tables set in a hidden garden of lavender, geraniums and tubs of herbs, it's a secret getaway for a cup of mint tea (picked from the garden, of course) and slice of homemade cake.

123 Regent's Park Road
NW1 8BE
Tel 0207 722 3999
www.tannrokka.com

3✷PRIMROSE BAKERY

With its sunny canary-yellow frontage, pale green walls and strings of bunting hanging over the counter, this gorgeous cupcake specialist is a very happy place to be. Trays of mouth-watering cakes are lined up in the counter cabinet—and not just any old flavours. Choose from the likes of peanut butter or delicately pale mauve Earl Grey, then sit at one of the 1950s Formica tables with a cup of tea and enjoy.

69 Gloucester Avenue
NW1 8LD
Tel 0207 483 4222
www.primrose-bakery.co.uk

5✷THE LITTLE ONE

It's worth walking to the far end of Regent's Park Road, away from the shops, to find this tiny coffee hangout. Tucked into the old office space of the antique shop next door—the vintage lights are for sale, courtesy of the neighbours—it's a chic retreat from the bustle of the rest of the street. The house specialties are crêpes (calorie-conscious locals love the spinach and carrot versions) and homemade breads. Get in early, though—most things are sold out by 2 pm.

115 Regent's Park Road
NW1 8UR

6✳ THE LANSDOWNE

Why can't every neighbourhood have a local pub like the Lansdowne? The airy main room is everything you want a laid-back drinking and eating destination to be. With big wooden tables, a lovely old pressed-plaster ceiling, metal jugs of flowers on the counter and a blackboard menu, it's hard to think of a better place for a lazy weekend afternoon. Unfussy and with great food; the perfect combination.
90 Gloucester Avenue
NW1 8HX
Tel 0207 483 0409
www.thelansdownepub.co.uk

7✳ YORK & ALBANY

This elegant pub, restaurant and hotel, part of Gordon Ramsay's empire, occupies an 1820s, Grade II listed, John Nash-designed building on the edge of Regent's Park. It's a very civilised spot for a stop-off. Pop in just for breakfast or a coffee before hitting the Primrose Hill shops, or for a drink and dinner at the end of the day. The lovely main bar has high ceilings with intricate cornicing, parquet floors and a long stainless steel bar topped with huge flower arrangements. Settle back into one of the elegant grey velvet armchairs and relax. Overnight guests are well looked after in gorgeous rooms kitted out with chandeliers, gilt mirrors, old Turkish carpets and some of the most comfortable mattresses in London. Before you leave, duck into Nonna's Deli next door. Created in the building's original stables, its rough brick floor and rustic charms offset the smart main building beautifully. And the takeaway coffee is great.
127–129 Parkway
NW1 7PS
Tel 0207 387 5700
www.gordonramsay.com

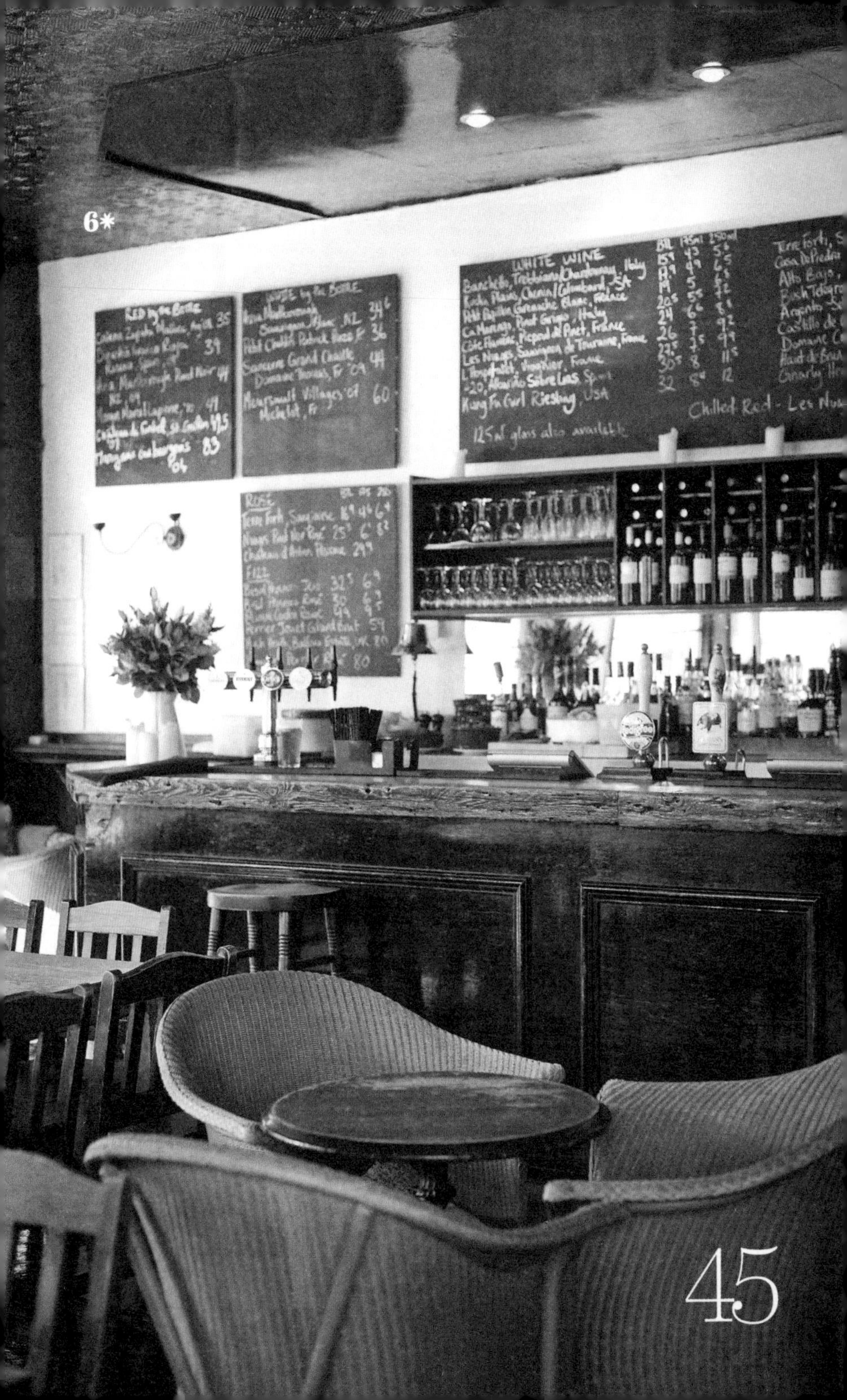

6*

nick selby
& ian james

Far too stylish to be called just a grocer's, Melrose and Morgan is a deli cum café cum kitchen that's a foodie's heaven. Not only are owners Nick Selby and Ian James passionate about food, but they have CVs that encompass photography, fashion and theatre, which explains the shop's stylish visual appeal. Set in a funky, modern space of bricks and glass, it's crammed with temptations. A table is piled high with homemade cakes like cherry pies and giant meringues, while the fridge is stocked with home-baked pies that even come in their own baking tin (so you can pass them off as your own!). Pop in for a coffee and leave with a jar of local Regent's Park honey.

Melrose and Morgan
42 Gloucester Avenue ❀ **NW1 8JD** ❀ **0207 722 0011** ❀ *www.melroseandmorgan.com*

'We love seeing art and films, especially at the Barbican'

How would you define London style?
It's diverse just by the nature of all the different age groups, professions, cultures and nationalities that live here.

Where do you go in London to be inspired?
It used to be art galleries and photographic exhibitions. Nowadays it's a trip to Selfridges food hall (www.selfridges.com), to keep up with food trends, or a trip to Borough Market (www.boroughmarket.org.uk) and **Maltby Street** (see page 50) to see what's on offer south of the river. We still love seeing art and films though, especially at the Barbican (www.barbican.org.uk).

Your favourite local places?
Our friend Claire Ptak runs **Violet** (see page 132) around the corner from where we live in London Fields. She sells great coffee from **Coleman Coffee Roasters** (see page 60) and the gingerbread is delicious—we are addicted.

Describe your perfect out-and-about weekend?

We work most weekends, as it's our busiest time. But it would definitely involve supper with friends on Saturday night at **Pizza East** (see page 161), then a walk through **Columbia Road Flower Market** (see page 98) on Sunday, then down Brick Lane (www.visitbricklane.org) and into Spitalfields Market (www.spitalfields. co.uk) for a browse. We usually end up at the Whitechapel Gallery (www. whitechapelgallery.org) for some culture and a bite to eat.

What's in your secret shopping address book?

For clothes, Albam in Islington (www.albamclothing.com); the clothes are very well made and they use interesting fabrics. For food, Leila's Shop in Shoreditch (15–17 Calvert Avenue, E2 7JP, tel 0207 729 9789). It's the best grocery shop in London: fantastic breads, wonderful cured meats from Poland and a superb selection of vegetables. For the bathroom, Aēsop in Shoreditch (www.aesop.com), especially for its geranium shower gel; and for books, **Daunt Books** on Marylebone High Street (see page 215). We love this old-fashioned bookshop and it's on our favourite high street.

Where's the best place for a weekend supper?

For a treat we would go to The Boundary (www.theboundary.co.uk). It's in the basement, but still has huge, high ceilings studded with old silver serving trays; very theatrical. The service is impeccable and the roast sirloin beef is the best in town. Then for something more casual, we will queue for our supper at **Spuntino** in Soho (see page 274), or the excellent grill at Barrafina, also in Soho (www.barrafina. co.uk); both are well worth the wait.

Best place for a drink?

The bar at **St John** on St John Street (see page 85). They also serve great bar snacks like smoked sprats with horseradish and the best cheese on toast.

Your favourite breakfast spot?

The bacon sandwich at St John Bread and Wine in Spitalfields (www. stjohngroup.uk.com/spitalfields) should not be missed, followed by a custard doughnut, if you can fit one in.

Where do you go in London to relax?

A walk through Regent's Park normally does the trick.

Top three things that every visitor to London should do?

See some great art at the Tate Modern (www.tate.org.uk), then a walk over the Millennium Bridge to St Paul's (www. stpauls.co.uk) and visit the Whispering Gallery. Then have lunch in nearby Clerkenwell at **The Modern Pantry** (see page 89), where Anna Hanson serves up brilliantly tasty fusion food all day long.

SHOP

1 St John Bakery Company
2 Bea's of Bloomsbury
3 Topolski
4 KäseSwiss
5 Jacob's Ladder Farms
6 Tayshaw
7 Hansen & Lydersen
8 Comptoir Gourmand
9 Little Bird
10 The Ham & Cheese Company
11 The Kernel Brewery
12 Fern Verrow
13 The Little Bread Pedlar
14 Coleman Coffee Roasters
15 Monmouth Coffee Company
16 Mons Cheese
17 Aubert & Mascoli

EAT & DRINK

18 40 Maltby Street
19 José and Pizarro

● Tube Station

Tower Hill

❋ TOWER OF LONDON ❋

Tower Bridge

River Thames

Jamaica Rd

Druid St

Bermondsey St

Stanworth St

6

bermondsey

1
2
3
4
5

Tower Bridge Rd

Riley Rd

Maltby St

18

7 8
9

● Bermonds

16
17

Abbey St

Spa Terminus

10 11 12 13 14
15

Grange Rd

bermondsey

This part of London will never win prizes for prettiness, but it's rapidly becoming a foodie mecca. What started as a tiny cluster around Maltby Street has spread to the nearby Spa Terminus area (www.spa-terminus.co.uk), and is now a hub of some of London's finest suppliers. Don't be put off by the industrial-estate surrounds. The railway arches along Maltby Street, Ropewalk, Stanworth Street, Druid Street—and now the Spa Terminus—house a collective of passionate retailers who put the nearby Borough Market to shame. While Borough has become more a tourist hotspot than a place to do your weekly shop, what has been christened Maltby Street Market is the real deal. Most companies here use the space under the arches as the weekday base for their wholesale businesses, only opening to the public on a Saturday morning (9 am–2 pm). So, skip the crowds at Borough, and come here instead.

1✳ ST JOHN BAKERY COMPANY

Chef Fergus Henderson is one of London's favourite restaurateurs and this is the baking arm of his business, headed up by baker Justin Piers Gellatly. (see page 85 for his flagship St John restaurant). During the week, the bread made here supplies Henderson's three restaurants as well as other food shops, but on a Saturday morning it opens to the public. Things are kept simple—a concrete floor, corrugated-iron roof and a table piled high with some of Britain's best bread. Sourdoughs, ryes and soda bread are quickly snapped up, but it is the company's custard doughnuts and mini Eccles cakes that really draw the crowds.
Arch 72, Druid Street
London SE1 2HQ
www.stjohngroup.uk.com/bakery

2✳ BEA'S OF BLOOMSBURY

Next door to the St John Bakery Company, the railway arch space has been hung with floral bunting, some chairs and tables set up and a pretty cake shop atmosphere created. Once again, there's no fancy fitout—a simple tabletop set up with wares—but the creations are so enticing that you'll want to take your pick and linger with a cup of coffee. How to choose from a pile of giant meringues in chocolate and strawberry flavours, cupcakes, lemon slices and mouthwatering peanut butter and jam slices? Buy one for now, and one to take away.
Arch 76, Druid Street
London SE1 2HQ
www.beasofbloomsbury.com

Terschelling
Schapenkaas

Organic, pasteurised
sheeps milk gouda made with
vegetarian rennet.
Handmade on the   £28.50
Island of Terschelling   per kg

3✳ TOPOLSKI
4✳ KÄSESWISS
5✳ JACOB'S LADDER FARMS

Keep heading down Druid Street and you'll find the arch occupied by Polish produce importers **Topolski**. Don't leave without buying some of their hot smoked sausages (flavoured with the likes of marjoram, caraway and juniper), and a jar of beetroot with horseradish to serve on the side. In the same arch is **KäseSwiss**, specialising in traditional farmhouse cheeses from Switzerland, such as gruyère, emmental and gouda with cumin, and also **Jacob's Ladder Farms**, selling meat from a collective of Sussex farms. Get to the meat counter early and you'll also find bread baked by local breadmaker Andy, in his Brixton home. He only makes about ten loaves a week to sell here, using a 1950s flour mill in his kitchen and a wood-fired oven in his back garden, and they sell out fast.
Arch 104, Druid Street
SE1 2HQ
www.kaseswiss.com, www.
jacobsladderfarms.co.uk

6✳ TAYSHAW

A huge arch space packed with an incredible variety of fruit and veg. An ex-Borough Market favourite, expect to find queues for the like of new-season girolle mushrooms, heritage tomatoes and short-season white asparagus. One of the area's busiest businesses.
Arch 60, Druid Street
London SE1 2EZ

7*

8*

8*

9* little bird

london dry gin

5 · Cocktails
5 · G&Ts
25 · Bottles to fly

tweet us @ littlebirdgin

ROPEWALK
7✳ HANSEN & LYDERSEN
8✳ COMPTOIR GOURMAND
9✳ LITTLE BIRD

Turn right off Druid Street, head beneath the railway line and you'll find the buzzing street market that has sprung up along Ropewalk. What started as a cluster of food producers selling direct to the public is now a busy stretch of bars and takeaway food stalls—causing some of the original inhabitants to move to nearby Spa Terminus. The crowds here are more interested in a gin and tonic and a snack than doing their weekly food shop. (Not that there's anything wrong with that.) That said, there are some gems amongst the more mainstream stalls. At **Hansen & Lydersen** (www.hansen-lydersen.com), you'll find smoked salmon that will make you forget any other smoked salmon you have ever tasted. The fourth-generation Norwegian company uses only sustainably harvested fish from the Norwegian Sea and the North Atlantic, hand-filleting and hand-salting the salmon before smoking it in a blend of juniper and beechwood in their smokehouse in Stoke Newington, north London. Nibble on a piece of salmon on sourdough as you shop, and buy a side to take home. **Comptoir Gourmand** (www. comptoirgourmand.co.uk) is a carboholic's paradise, and there's always a queue at the patisserie boulangerie's tables, piled with homemade French pastries. The sausage brioche is particularly unmissable. As for that gin and tonic, the **Little Bird** (www. littlebirdgin.com) can oblige. Selling its own blend of London Dry Gin, you can stop for a cocktail, and buy a £25 bottle to take home. Cheers.
Ropewalk
SE1 3PA
www.maltby.st

10✳ THE HAM & CHEESE COMPANY

The Ham & Cheese Company has decamped from Ropewalk to larger premises in Spa Terminus, which means even more temptations to choose from. You'll find charcuterie and cheese sourced from small, independent suppliers in France and Italy and then matured underneath the railway arches. The damp brickwork and cool temperatures provide ideal conditions, apparently. There's also unpasteurised olives, olive oil and Italian rice and pasta on offer.

Spa Terminus, Arch 10
Dockley Road Industrial Estate
Dockley Road
SE16 3SF
Tel 07970 532 485
www.thehamandcheeseco.com

11✳ THE KERNEL BREWERY

Next door to The Ham & Cheese Company, brewer Evin O'Riordain creates and bottles his award-winning pale ales and stouts at The Kernal Brewery. Grab a bottle, a few slices of something tasty from The Ham & Cheese Company and that's lunch sorted. Delicious.

Spa Terminus, Arch 11
Dockley Road Industrial Estate
Dockley Road
SE16 3SF
Tel 0207 231 4516
www.thekernelbrewery.com

12* FERN VERROW

On the Spa Terminus industrial estate, you'll find farmer Jane Scotter selling seasonal produce from her biodynamic Fern Verrow farm on the border of Wales and Herefordshire. Look for unusual varieties that never make it to supermarket shelves, as well as homemade jams and vinegars using up excess produce that might otherwise go to waste, like strawberry vinegar made from a berry glut.

Spa Terminus, Unit 10
Dockley Road Industrial Estate
Dockley Road
SE1 3SF
Tel 01981 510 288
www.fernverrow.com

13* THE LITTLE BREAD PEDLAR
14* COLEMAN COFFEE ROASTERS

Rated by fellow Spa Terminus neighbours as sellers of the best croissants in the area, this squeezy industrial unit does a brisk trade in all things doughy. And yes, the handmade croissants are good. **The Little Bread Pedlar** delivers its wares by bicycle to eateries across London (including **La Fromagerie**, see page 222 and **The Ace** hotel, see page 165), but it's here that the baking magic happens. The tiny space is shared with **Coleman Coffee Roasters**, purveyors of one of the best flat whites in London. A fresh pastry and coffee to go—what's not to love?

Spa Terminus
Unit 5, Dockley Road Industrial Estate
Dockley Road, SE16 3SF
www.lbpedlar.com
www.colemancoffee.com

15* MONMOUTH COFFEE COMPANY

One of London's favourite coffee companies and an early adopter of the Maltby Street area, their new Spa Terminus shop is tricky to find—down a narrow alleyway and wedged between the railway line and an apartment block. But if coffee is your thing, seek it out. Buy yourself some beans and a takeaway coffee for your food shopping wandering.

Arch 3, Spa North
Between Dockley Road and Spa Road
SE16 4RP
www.monmouthcoffee.co.uk

13*

14*

13*

16* MONS CHEESE
17* AUBERT & MASCOLI

It doesn't get more French than cheese importers **Mons**. Founded in the 1960s by Hubert Mons, and now run by his sons Laurent and Hervé, this archway houses a temple to the very best fromage you can buy—all of it French, of course (with one or two Swiss exceptions allowed to sneak in). Most of the cheeses are ripened in the Mons cellars in the East Loire, although some mature on the Bermondsey site. Conveniently, the archway is shared with organic-wine importers **Aubert & Mascoli**. A bottle of smooth red to go with your cheese? *Mais oui.*
Unit 2, Voyager Business Park
SE16 4RP
Tel 0207 064 6912
www.mons-cheese.co.uk
www.aubertandmascoli.com

18* 40 MALTBY STREET

A glass of wine and a spot of lunch at this archway winebar is the perfect end to a morning of Maltby Street meandering. Sharing its archway with an importer of natural wines from small-scale producers in France, Italy, Spain and Slovenia, 40 Maltby Street offers a daily-changing menu to go with the liquid refreshments. The likes of pork and prune terrine and cuttlefish on toast are the perfect accompaniment to a carefully considered wine list. Not flashy, but worth a visit—check the website, as opening hours are limited.
40 Maltby Street
SE1 3PA
Tel 0207 237 9247
www.40maltbystreet.com

josé pizarro

No visit to Bermondsey is complete without dropping into the restaurants owned by Spanish chef José Pizarro: corner tapas bar José, and the larger Pizarro. Lucky locals to have these buzzy places in their midst. The smaller José is constantly packed (you can't book), serving deliciously authentic tapas, washed down with Spanish wines and sherries, all in a funky setting of exposed brickwork and marble counter tops. Find a stool if you can (stand up if you can't) and enjoy the vibe. Two hundred metres down the road at Pizarro, with its booths and private dining room, you'll hopefully get a seat! Dishes are larger than the small tapas served at José, but the mood is still one of sharing delicious food with friends and enjoying cava, wine and sherries from independent Spanish producers.

JOSÉ AND PIZARRO
❀ **José** ❀ **104 Bermondsey Street SE1 3UB**
❀ **Pizarro** ❀ **194 Bermondsey Street SE1 3TQ** ❀ *www.josepizarro.com* ❀ **0207 378 9455**

'Maltby Street is a hotbed of the coolest new food suppliers'

How would you define London style?
London is the best city in the world—chic, stylish and where it all happens.

Where do you go to be inspired?
I love standing on the Millennium Bridge. Look one way and you have St Paul's and the Tower of London—two of the most beautiful old buildings in London. Look the other way and you have the Tate Modern and the London Eye. Awe-inspiring.

Your favourite local places?
Maltby Street (see page 50) is a hotbed of the coolest new food suppliers and restaurants. I also love eating at Zucca in Bermondsey Street (www.zuccalondon.com), because the food is wonderfully fresh and seasonal, and every time I go I am surprised by the menu and flavours.

Describe your perfect out-and-about weekend?
On Saturday I wake early and head to Billingsgate (www.billingsgatefishmarket.org) to pick up some fish. Then I go for coffee at Monmouth (www.monmouthcoffee.co.uk) in Borough Market, followed by food shopping

PRAWNS, CHILLI, GARLIC

MACKEREL, ORANGE, BLACK OLIVES

WHITEBAITS, FRIED EGG, PIQUILLO PE

GIROLLES, RED ONIONS, MANCHEGO

SQUID, RUNNER BEANS

RAZOR CLAMS, CHORIZO, MINT

CHICKEN LIVERS, FINO

IBERICO PORK FILLET

CLAMS, TOMATO, JAMÓN

PADRON PEPPERS

with friends. Sundays are very lazy days
for me. I'll pop into José for a glass of fino
before heading to Roka in Canary Wharf
(www.rokarestaurant.com) for dim sum,
my favourite thing to eat on Sunday.

What's in your secret shopping address book?

Maltby Street (see page 50) for bread,
vegetables and cheese. I love O'Shea's
in Bermondsey (www.osheasbutchers.
com) for meat, and Selfridges (www.
selfridges.com) does a wonderful selection
of Maldonado hams. Iberica near Oxford
Circus (www.ibericalondon.co.uk) is great
for Spanish delicacies.

Where's the best place for a weekend supper?

Apart from my restaurants, Zucca
(www.zuccalondon.com), Le Caprice
(www.le-caprice.co.uk) or **Pizza East** (see
page 161). Zucca and Le Caprice because
they're just so classy and 'English', and
Pizza East because it's so much fun. It's
always lively and buzzing, and the pizza
flavours are wonderful.

Best place for a drink?

Lounge Bohemia in Shoreditch (1E Great
Eastern Street, London EC2A 3EJ, tel
07720 707 000). Just such a cool venue,
and the cocktails are delicious and
really creative.

Your favourite breakfast spot?

The Wolseley (www.thewolseley.com)
because it's a stunning place to sit and
eat really traditional English food.
Wonderful teas, too.

Top three things that every visitor to London should do?

Go to the National Gallery (www.
nationalgallery.org.uk), Tate Modern
(www.tate.org.uk) and the Anchor
& Hope pub in Southwark (www.
anchorandhopepub.co.uk) for a proper
pint and wonderful food.

65

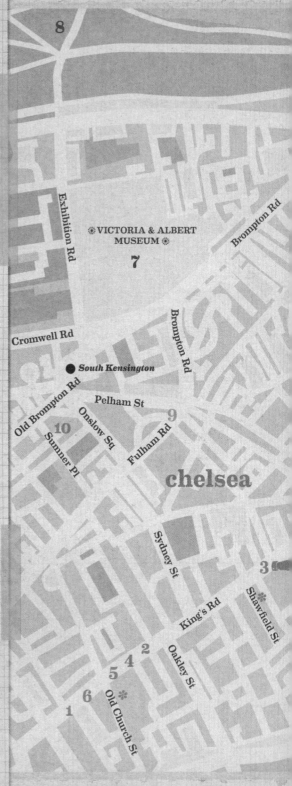

SHOP

1 *Rococo Chocolates*
2 *Green & Stone*
3 *Jo Loves*
4 *Sigmar*
5 *Designers Guild*
6 *The Shop at Bluebird*
✻ *British Red Cross*
✻ *Oxfam*

EAT & DRINK

7 *Victoria & Albert Museum Café*

8 *The Serpentine Sackler Gallery*

EAT, DRINK & SHOP

9 *The Conran Shop*

SLEEP

10 *Number Sixteen*

● *Tube Station*

✻ DESIGNER CHARITY

Special mention to two of London's best charity shops, both well worth a look for a designer bargain. The **British Red Cross** shop, tucked down a King's Road side street, is famed for its haul of big-name vintage and new labels. Sign up to the mailing list for the annual designer evening, with special donations from the likes of Chanel and Dolce & Gabbana. *69–71 Old Church Street, SW3 5BS. Tel 0207 376 7300. www.redcross.org.uk*
At the branch of **Oxfam** further down the King's Road, you might find a Chanel bag or a pair of Prada shoes. With its old parquet floors and funky display cabinets, the shop is more like a designer boutique than a charity outlet. It's definitely worth popping in. *123a Shawfield Street, King's Road, SW3 4PL. Tel 0207 351 7979. www.oxfam.org.uk*

chelsea & south kensington

It may be a shadow of its former swinging sixties self—too many same old, same old high street chains—but the King's Road still has a lot to offer. Start your stroll at World's End for the most interesting shops. As you head towards Sloane Square, things become a bit more predictable. Better to take a detour into nearby South Kensington, with its beautifully leafy residential streets and pockets of interesting shops. This is one of the most polished areas of London, and just meandering around its streets is a lovely way to spend an afternoon. Think of it as lifestyle window-shopping.

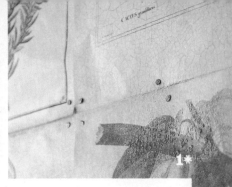

1✳ ROCOCO CHOCOLATES

Opened in 1983, this chocoholics' paradise was one of the first purveyors of the kind of luxury, unusual chocolates that are now commonplace, but no one does it better than Rococo. And no one has a prettier shop. Old botanical prints adorn the walls, a chandelier hangs from the ceiling and trays of handmade delicacies are displayed in an old-fashioned cabinet. Elsewhere, shelves are stacked with gorgeously wrapped bars, with flavours such as orange and geranium dark milk and sea salt milk chocolate, while pretty, ribboned boxes are stacked on a dresser. One hundred per cent temptation.

321 King's Road
SW3 5EP
Tel 0207 352 5857
www.rococochocolates.com

2✳ GREEN & STONE

A Chelsea institution, Green & Stone has been selling art materials here since 1934. Whether you're an amateur or a professional, it's a pleasure just to browse the crammed shelves. Old plan chests are filled with any and every type of paper; you'll find gold leaf, paints, pencils—whatever your creative heart desires. The shop itself is given a delightfully higgledy-piggledy atmosphere by the sloping, worn wooden floors and piled-high merchandise. If anywhere is going to inspire you to get creative, this place is it.

259 King's Road
SW3 5EL
Tel 0207 352 0837
www.greenandstone.com

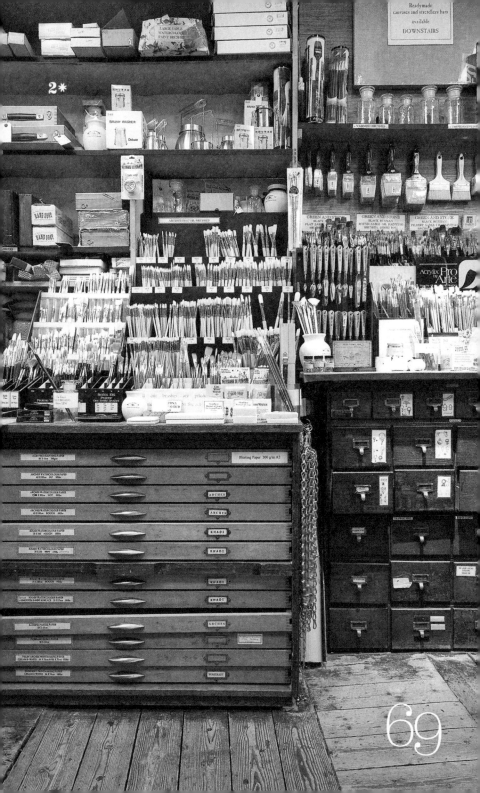

69

3✱ JO LOVES

One of the prettiest shopping streets in London is home to the first stand-alone shop from fragrance guru, Jo Malone. The woman who created one of the world's best-loved beauty brands, then sold it to global giant Estée Lauder, is doing it all again with her new business, Jo Loves. And it's just as delicious second time round. As for the shop itself, exquisite. A 16-year-old Jo had her first job in this very spot when it was a florist's, so the space has special meaning for her. It's dominated by a dramatic red 'fragrance tapas' bar, for customers to sit and choose their favourite scents. Jo's vision of a brasserie, but with bath oils and body creams to be sniffed and tested instead of sipping drinks, is an unmissable experience for beauty fans. And with fragrances as good as her classic Pomelo, you're unlikely to leave empty-handed.

42 Elizabeth Street
SW1W 9NZ
Tel 0207 730 8611
www.joloves.com

4✱ SIGMAR

The owner's single-minded passion for beautifully made, classic furniture shines through in this small, sleek shop. The stock is from a mix of eras, but it's unified by its simple, tasteful style. Nineteenth-century wooden chairs sit alongside 21st-century light fittings and perfectly crafted oak tables that were designed fifty years ago, but look modern today. No clutter, just a careful edit of very good taste, set against the shop's pale grey walls and polished wood floor. Lovely.

236 King's Road
SW3 5EL
Tel 0207 751 5801
www.sigmarlondon.com

4*

5✳ DESIGNERS GUILD

If your taste in homewares tends towards minimalism, then step away from this shop. If, however, you love colour, pattern and vibrancy, come on in. Every surface is decorated with stripes, flowers and geometric designs, and you can't help but be put in a positive mood. Blending in with the home accessories are handpicked pieces of vintage furniture, like a 1950s chair reupholstered in bold green tweed, or an old teak side table with a bright-yellow laminated top. The mix of old and new is perfectly judged. If you're not a colour convert by the time you leave, then you never will be.

267–277 King's Road
SW3 5EN
Tel 0207 351 5775
www.designersguild.com

6✳ THE SHOP AT BLUEBIRD

Housed in a cavernous Art Deco garage, this lifestyle shop is a seductive blend of high-end designer and quirky, affordable buys. It's hard to think where else a tube of cinnamon toothpaste would be displayed alongside an £1800 YSL dress. It's a magical mix. The space itself is worth a look; it's huge. Enter through a café on the old garage forecourt and you're into a warehouse-sized room of womenswear, menswear, antique furnishings, books, magazines, artworks—and the odd tube of toothpaste. There's even a spa. Get your eyebrows threaded or spend £3800 on an antique French mirror; the choice is yours.

350 King's Road
SW3 5UU
Tel 0207 351 3873
www.theshopatbluebird.com

7✳ VICTORIA & ALBERT MUSEUM CAFÉ

It may be one of the world's great museums, but the V&A also has a hidden gem—one of London's most ornate cafés. Not just that, it was the first museum restaurant in the world, built in the 1860s to show off British design and craftsmanship. As entry to the museum is free, you can come for coffee at the V&A without feeling you ought to check out the art, although the glorious Victorian decor in the café is an experience in itself. There are three rooms to choose from: Morris, Gamble and Poynter. In the Morris room, created by designer William Morris's decorating company, you'll find theatrical stained glass and wonderfully tiled sweeping arches. In Gamble, the walls are covered in ceramic tiles and the ceiling in enamelled iron, all richly patterned and ornate. The Poynter room's colour scheme of blue and white is inspired by Dutch artists. London's most OTT coffee stop.

Cromwell Road
SW7 2RL
Tel 0207 942 2000
www.vam.ac.uk

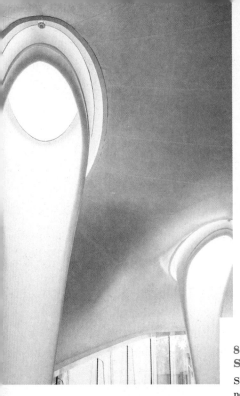

8✳ THE SERPENTINE SACKLER GALLERY

Star architect Zaha Hadid finally has a permanent structure in central London. Her transformation and extension of an 1805 Grade II heritage-listed former gunpowder store has created one of the most intriguing galleries and cafés in the capital. The Serpentine Sackler Gallery stands on the north side of the Serpentine pond in Hyde Park. The original building is elegant in its own right, but it's the Hadid touches that make it worth visiting. The gallery interior has been reworked, and an extraordinary futuristic extension added, housing The Magazine restaurant. If the gallery's contemporary artwork doesn't appeal, a cup of tea amidst Hadid's creamy, curved, elongated columns is a show-stopper. It's like a spaceship has landed in the middle of the park and is crawling over the historic brickwork of the original gallery, slowly engulfing it. London had to wait a while, but Hadid's vision is well worth it.

West Carriage Drive
Kensington Gardens
W2 2AR
Tel 0207 298 7552
www.serpentinegalleries.org/restaurant

9 ✳ THE CONRAN SHOP

Housed in the decorative 1909 building
that was once the headquarters of the
Michelin Tyre Company, this has to be
one of London's most impressive shop
settings. Even if you're not interested in
the furniture shopping inside, come for a
glass of champagne and a platter of *fruits
de mer* in the Bibendum Oyster Bar—
named after Michelin's iconic Monsieur
Bibendum, the cheekily chubby 'Michelin
Man'. Set in the shop's beautifully tiled
forecourt, it's an elegant spot to rest after
a hard day's shopping.
Michelin House
81 Fulham Road
SW3 6RD
Tel 0207 589 7401
www.conranshop.co.uk

kit kemp

Hotelier Kit Kemp is the woman behind some of London's best boutique hotels. Together with her husband Tim, she owns Firmdale Hotels, with eight London establishments, including new hotspot Ham Yard, just behind Piccadilly. Her touch is unmistakeable: an intoxicating and playful blend of art, colour and pattern, combined with the highest levels of luxury and service. No wonder her creations, including the Soho, Covent Garden and Charlotte Street hotels, are some of the most popular in the capital.

Number Sixteen is the most bijou of the group, tucked into a Victorian terraced house in a residential street in South Kensington. A short stroll from the Victoria & Albert and Natural History Museums, as well as the shops of Knightsbridge and the greenery of Kensington Gardens, it's also blessed with one of London's prettiest hotel gardens. The perfect place to stay.

Number Sixteen
16 Sumner Place SW7 3EG ❖ **Tel 0207 589 5232** ❖ **www.firmdale.com**

'I love ballet, and the old Covent Garden Market with its street entertainment'

How would you define London style?
English eccentric.

Where do you go in London to be inspired?
London is like a collection of villages, and I am part of South Kensington where I live, with all its beautiful white stucco buildings. I like the fact that London is so green with its many parks. I walk to work every day from home, which is near the Royal Albert Hall (www.royalalberthall.com). I always go down Exhibition Road, past the Science Museum (www.sciencemuseum.org.uk) and the Natural History Museum (www.nhm.ac.uk), which is my favourite building in London.

Your favourite local places?
The Victoria & Albert Reading Rooms (www.vandareadingrooms.co.uk) and Mint (www.mintshop.co.uk)—a great shop where you can always find something different and quirky.

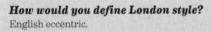

Describe your perfect out-and-about weekend?

I go to the country every weekend, but if I was in London then it would involve walking around the Covent Garden area, including Long Acre and Neal Street, for the different shops and street life, going to the Royal Opera House (www.roh.org.uk) as I love ballet, and the old Covent Garden Market with its street entertainment and attractions.

What's in your secret shopping address book?

Talisman (www.talismanlondon.com) for a fabulous selection of unique mid-20th-century furniture and 18th-century continental antiques. Tissus d'Hélène at Chelsea Harbour (www.tissusdhelene.co.uk) for designer fabrics and wallpapers from Europe and America. Bloomsbury Flowers (www.bloomsburyflowers.co.uk) put together some of the most beautiful flower arrangements in London. The owners are both ex-Royal Ballet School dancers and supply the flowers for the Royal Opera House. And St Paul's (www.actorschurch.org) has wonderful Orpheus Foundation concerts and recitals.

Where's the best place for a weekend supper?

Brasserie Max at the Covent Garden Hotel. Or for a very simple meal, Ikeda (www.ikedarestaurant.co.uk), my favourite Japanese restaurant in London. I love sitting at the counter watching them cook exquisite things.

Best place for a drink?

I love the Rose Bakery in **Dover Street Market** (see page 282) for tea and carrot cake.

Your favourite breakfast spot?

The café at the Serpentine (www.serpentinebarandkitchen.com) in Hyde Park, as I like to watch the swimmers in the morning.

Favourite cultural sights?

The Royal Opera House (I love going to the ballet, not only for the amazing performances but for the beautiful building and wonderful sets), the Sir John Soane's Museum (www.soane.org), and the Wallace Collection (www.wallacecollection.org).

Top three things that every visitor to London should do?

Take a Boris Bike (London's cycle rental scheme, nicknamed for the city's mayor, www.tfl.gov.uk) to the Tate Modern (www.tate.org.uk), and then cycle along the South Bank and pop over the bridge to Somerset House (www.somersethouse.org.uk), where you can ice skate in the winter or look at the art and cultural exhibitions. Pack a picnic to have in St James's Park. And go to the Royal Opera House and watch ballet or an opera, and have a very relaxed supper in the Paul Hamlyn Hall to look at all the surroundings in the interval.

SHOP

1 *Clerkenwell Tales*
2 *EC One*
3 *The Family Business*

EAT & DRINK

4 *St John Bar & Restaurant*
5 *J+A Café*
6 *The Quality Chop House*
7 *Caravan*
8 *Morito*
9 *The Modern Pantry*

EAT, DRINK & SLEEP

10 *The Zetter Townhouse*
11 *Fox & Anchor*

● *Tube Station*
● *Train Station*

Angel

City Rd

Goswell Rd

Rosebery Ave

Exmouth Market

2

3

7 1 8

6

Bowling Green Ln

Farringdon Rd

Old St

9 5

10

Clerkenwell Rd

St John St

clerkenwell

4

11 Barbican

Farringdon

Charterhouse St

SMITHFIELD
MARKET

Chancery Lane

clerkenwell

From the Grade II listed Victorian splendour of Smithfield meat market, through history-soaked cobbled squares and laneways, to the pedestrianised charm of Exmouth Market, this is one of the most picturesque pockets of London. Clerkenwell has been a hub of activity since the Middle Ages, when the clerks (clergymen) put on mystery plays at the site of the Clerks' Well in Farringdon Lane. These days, you're more likely to find architects, interior designers and other cool creatives, who gather at the area's many pubs and restaurants. But the cobbles are still there, as are many of the medieval buildings. If you love urban history, it's a part of London not to be missed.

1✳ CLERKENWELL TALES

Times are tough for the book trade, so
this independently owned shop is a rarity.
The owner prides himself on his careful
edit of fiction, art and design, culture
and politics, and London writing. The
shop also specialises in distinctively
beautiful books, especially graphic novels,
curating them like treasures on the shop's
streamlined shelves. No wonder David
One Day Nicholls regularly pops in
for a browse.
30 Exmouth Market
EC1R 4QE
Tel 0207 713 8135
www.clerkenwell-tales.co.uk

2✳ EC ONE

This independent jewellery shop
champions new designers as well as
creating bespoke pieces in its on-site
workshop. The result is a range that goes
above and beyond your average jewellery
shop, with items from the cheap and
quirky up to the grandly precious. The
passion for good design is clear, with a
constant stream of undiscovered names
showcased in the shop's annual graduate
design awards. You'll definitely find
something unusually special here.
41 Exmouth Market
EC1R 4QL
Tel 0207 713 6185
www.econe.co.uk

4*

4*

4*

4 ☀ ST JOHN BAR AND RESTAURANT

One of the first businesses to move in and turn Clerkenwell into the don't-miss destination it is today, St John is also one of London's most cutting-edge restaurants. It frequently tops the lists of chefs' favourite places to eat. Nose-to-tail dining is the philosophy in this former ham and bacon smokehouse. Go for the whole roast suckling pig to get the full experience. Decor is white, stripped-back and industrial looking—more like a photographer's studio than one of the most revered restaurants in London. Even if you just pop in for a drink at the bar, don't miss it.

26 St John Street
EC1M 4AY
Tel 0207 251 0848
www.stjohngroup.uk.com/smithfield

5 ☀ J+A CAFÉ

Sisters Aoife and Johanna Ledwidge have created a secret café oasis in this old diamond-cutting factory. You have to be in the know to find it, but it's worth seeking out. Walk down an alleyway and into a shady courtyard filled with tubs of geraniums and hung with bunting. Inside, exposed brick walls, an oversized blackboard and a large communal wooden table create a relaxed, friendly atmosphere. As for the food, soda bread and cakes are homemade daily, and ingredients are sourced from local suppliers where possible. If in doubt over the menu, order the roast chicken sandwich on white crusty bread; it's pretty unbeatable.

1–4 Sutton Lane
EC1M 5PU
Tel 0207 490 2992
www.jandacafe.com

6✳ THE QUALITY CHOP HOUSE

Built in 1869 as a lunch spot for working
men, this Grade II listed townhouse has
changed little since Victorian times. Just
as the early patrons did, diners sit on the
heritage-listed wooden pews and gaze at
the elegant wood panelling and ornate
chequered tile floor. What *has* changed is
the food: since its new owners took over
the restaurant and adjoining wine bar
at the end of 2012, there has been a non-
stop buzz about the meat-centric dishes.
Everything is made in-house (much
of it sold in the Food Shop & Butcher
next door), from the cured meats to the
brioche, and even some of the drinks,
such as damson gin and elderflower
vodka. Add the delightful, knowledgeable
service and you've got one of London's
most visit-worthy restaurants in the sort
of historically stunning setting that makes
this city so special. You'll be charmed.
88–94 Farringdon Road
EC1R 3EA
Tel 0207 278 1452
www.thequalitychophouse.com

7✳ CARAVAN

A great coffee is guaranteed at this busy
corner café. Beans are roasted on-site to
create one of the best cups in the capital,
but don't come just for the coffee. Join the
crowds who have made Caravan one of
London's favourite brunch spots, thanks
to its spot-on menu ('two crumpets and
too much butter'), cool decor and always-
friendly staff. Dinner is also worth a look.
With its rough concrete floor, reclamation
wood bar and huge glass industrial-esque
lights, the whole place has a funky,
laid-back feel that makes for a perfect
weekend morning of paper-reading
and people-watching.
11–13 Exmouth Market
EC1R 4QD
Tel 0207 833 8115
www.caravanonexmouth.co.uk

8✳ MORITO

London's hippest tapas bar is the rough-
and-ready younger sibling of the Moro
restaurant next door, and brings a little
slice of Spain to east London. With
the tiny space dominated by an orange
Formica counter and a few tables and
stools (no comfy dining chairs here), the
look is no-frills, but the food is anything
but. The place is always packed with
diners enjoying wine by the carafe and
food that takes your breath away. Don't
be put off by the strip lighting. This is one
of the most delicious spots in the area.
32 Exmouth Market
EC1R 4QE
Tel 0207 278 7007
www.morito.co.uk

9✳ THE MODERN PANTRY

On the same pretty cobbled square as **The Zetter Townhouse** (see page 90), The Modern Pantry is packed at all hours, thanks to its antipodean flavour combinations, chic interior and damn fine coffee. Chef Anna Hansen was raised in New Zealand, and her food shines with the sort of imagination taken for granted in the cafés of Auckland and Sydney, but rarely found in London. The sugar-cured New Caledonian prawn omelette, with green chilli, spring onion, coriander and smoked-chilli sambal, is, quite rightly, a legend in brunch circles. Set in a charmingly wonky Georgian townhouse, with bare wooden floors and a rickety staircase, the pale grey walls and sleek Scandi furniture ensure The Modern Pantry looks as elegantly contemporary as the food it serves. The southern hemisphere's loss is London's gain.

47–48 St John's Square
EC1V 4JJ
Tel 0207 553 9210
www.themodernpantry.co.uk

89

10✳ THE ZETTER TOWNHOUSE

The cocktail bar of this 13-bedroom Georgian townhouse hotel is the perfect place to begin or end an evening—or both. Tucked at the back of a cobbled square, there's no clue from the outside to the fantastical atmosphere within. Cross the threshold and you're into Dickens' *The Old Curiosity Shop*. Part apothecary, part gentleman's club, the bar is filled with potted palms, stag antlers, taxidermy, old framed prints and worn Turkish rugs. Settle back in a velvet Chesterfield sofa, or sink into an armchair upholstered with an old hessian sack. Then order a cocktail that nods to the area's Dickensian past of gin distilleries and debauchery. The martini even comes with a homemade citrus essence, dispensed into your drink with a glass pipette by the waiter. As for the bedrooms, they are sexy, fun and bijoux. Old fairground carousel signage is used as bedheads, there's boldly striped carpet, brightly painted walls and glam touches of gold mosaic tiling. It all makes for a very theatrical night out.

49–50 St John's Square
EC1V 4JJ
Tel 0207 324 4567
www.thezettertownhouse.com

11✱ FOX & ANCHOR

This pub with six bedrooms upstairs is a jewel of Victoriana. Beautifully restored, it's a perfect example of what a proper London boozer—as opposed to a tricked-up gastropub—should be. The mahogany panelling, Arts and Crafts era tiling, etched glass and moulded decorative ceiling create a room that has character in abundance. Sit up at the bar and wash down a homemade pork pie with a pint of London ale from an antique pewter tankard, or venture to the Fox's Den at the back of the pub, where dining tables are tucked away in their own cosy wood-panelled rooms. After a dinner of traditional British fare (homemade pies, oysters, perfectly cooked steak) you can venture upstairs to one of the elegant bedrooms. Soak in an oversized bath and then crawl into a supremely comfortable bed. One tip: take earplugs. The downside of a night in the heart of one of London's hippest neighbourhoods is the sound of its trendy young things partying the night away. Not even double glazing on the original lead windows can fix that.

115 Charterhouse Street
EC1M 6AA
Tel 0207 250 1300
www.foxandanchor.com

'After a dinner of traditional British fare (homemade pies, oysters, perfectly cooked steak), you can venture upstairs to one of the elegant bedrooms'

mo coppoletta

Prepare to have all your preconceived ideas about tattoo parlours challenged.
In The Family Business, the tattoo is treated as a 21st-century art form.
Step into a world of religious iconography, hand-painted framed design
illustrations and artists' portfolios, where the gentle hum of tattooing needles
comes from the studio at the back. Italian-born owner Mo Coppoletta—
creator of this temple to the tattoo—has collaborated with the likes of artist
Damien Hirst, and credits an early exposure to religious and decorative art
with drawing him into the tattoo business. Peruse the portfolios to choose
your artist, who will then create a bespoke design, just for you. It's a serious
business: you can book one of the many visiting international practitioners
who view a stint here as a rite of passage, but if you want to wait for Mo
himself, join the year-long queue.

THE FAMILY BUSINESS
58 Exmouth Market EC1R 4QE ✱ 0207 278 9526 ✱ *www.thefamilybusinesstattoo.com*

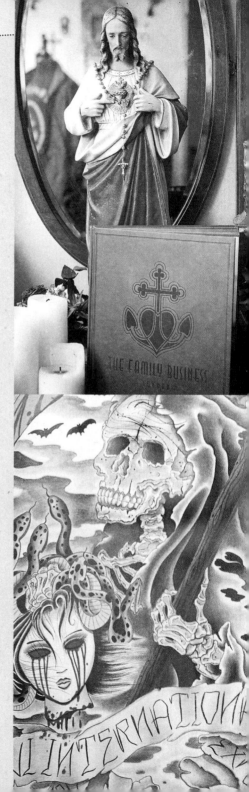

'I love paintings, and nothing is more inspiring than the National Gallery'

How would you define London style?
It's fresh and innovative, but timeless at the same time.

Where do you go in London to be inspired?
The National Portrait Gallery (www.npg.org.uk), The National Gallery (www.nationalgallery.org.uk) and Estorick Collection of Modern Italian Art (www.estorickcollection.com). I love paintings, and nothing is more inspiring than selecting a couple of rooms at the National Gallery and immersing myself in a few selected works at a time. Portraits are always so direct and pure. They have a lot of power. That's why I love the National Portrait Gallery. I'm also a big fan of the Futurist movement and Italian art from the first half of the 20th century, and the Estorick Collection is the perfect place for it.

Your favourite local places to eat?
The Eagle in Clerkenwell (159 Farringdon Road, EC1R 3AL, tel 0207 837 1353). I discovered The Eagle only recently and

wondered how I could have left the first-ever gastropub off my list of places for so long. Go for their signature steak sandwich.

What's in your secret shopping address book?
It's no secret—Saville Row in Mayfair. Spencer Hart (www.spencerhart.com) for his 1960s-inspired tailoring, and Lanvin (www.lanvin.com) all around.

Describe your perfect out-and-about weekend?
A stroll down to the South Bank Centre (www.southbankcentre.co.uk), or a jog in Hyde Park followed by a visit to the Serpentine (www.serpentinegallery.org) and dinner in one of the restaurants mentioned below.

Where's the best place for a weekend supper?
Roka (www.rokarestaurant.com) for oriental atmosphere, La Petite Maison (www.lpmlondon.co.uk) for a breeze of the French Riviera, or L'Anima (www.lanima.co.uk) for the finest Italian.

Best place for a drink?
The Connaught Bar in Mayfair (www.the-connaught.co.uk) for its sleek decor and exquisite drinks (the Bloody Mary is amazing), or 69 Colebrooke Row (www.69colebrookerow.com), which is London's best-kept secret. Here you can enjoy arguably the best drinks in the world. My friend Tony (the owner) is a genius.

Your favourite breakfast spot?
A good start to the day is an Italian cappuccino at Cecconi's (www.cecconis.co.uk) in Mayfair.

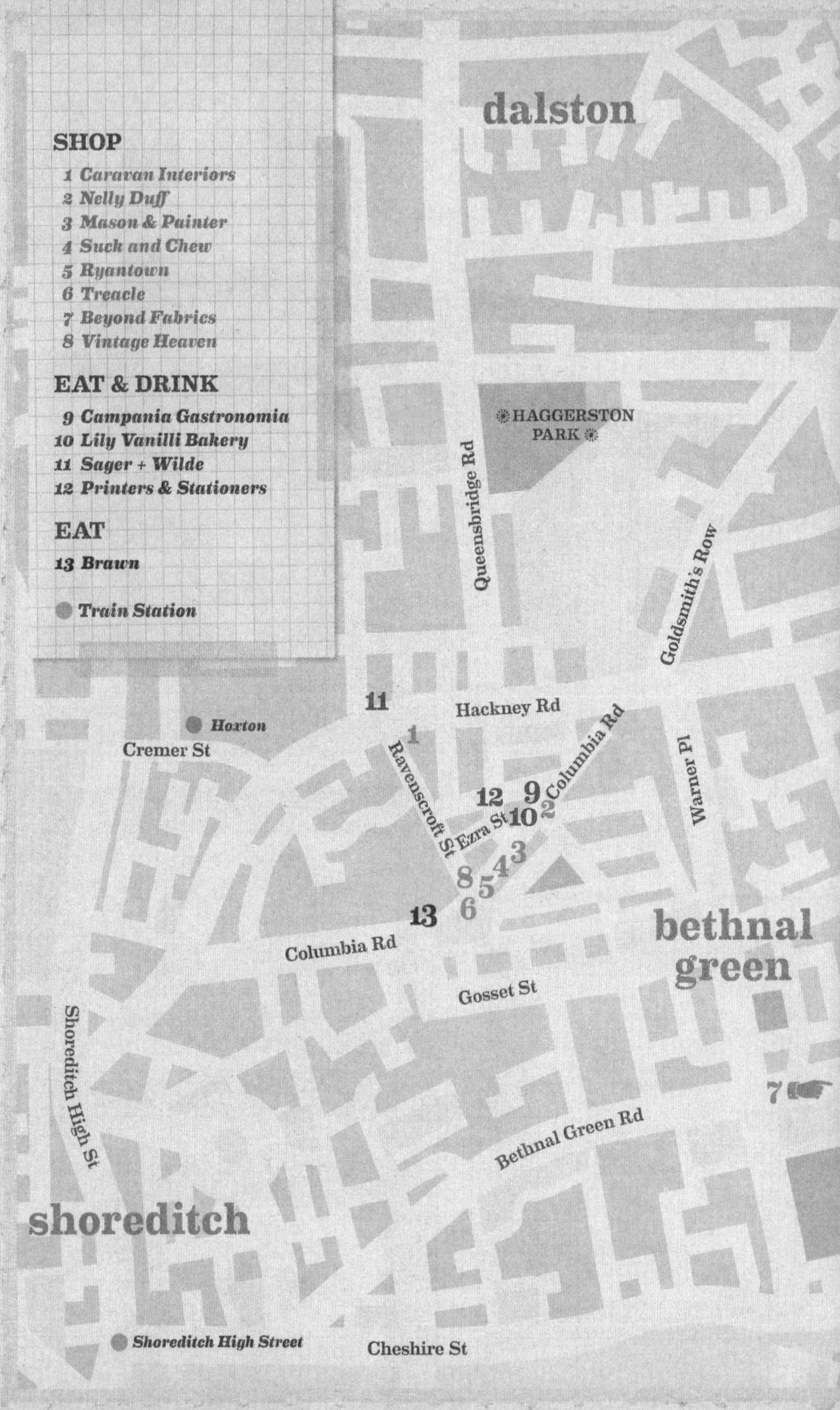

SHOP

1 *Caravan Interiors*
2 *Nelly Duff*
3 *Mason & Painter*
4 *Suck and Chew*
5 *Ryantown*
6 *Treacle*
7 *Beyond Fabrics*
8 *Vintage Heaven*

EAT & DRINK

9 *Campania Gastronomia*
10 *Lily Vanilli Bakery*
11 *Sager + Wilde*
12 *Printers & Stationers*

EAT

13 *Brawn*

● *Train Station*

dalston

● HAGGERSTON PARK ●

Queensbridge Rd

Goldsmith's Row

11

Hackney Rd

● Hoxton

Cremer St

1

Ravenscroft St

Columbia Rd

Warner Pl

12 9

Ezra St

10 2

8 4 3

5

13 6

bethnal green

Gosset St

7 ☞

Shoreditch High St

Bethnal Green Rd

shoreditch

● *Shoreditch High Street*

Cheshire St

Columbia rd

In an age of chain stores and lookalike high streets, *Columbia Road* is a magical spot. This tiny strip of independent shops comes alive only at weekends. Some of the shops are Sunday-only; when a flower market down the middle of the road draws the crowds, others open Saturday and Sunday, too. Call each shop individually to check their hours. On Sunday it gets very busy, but it's worth the squash. Come early and just wander, grabbing a coffee and some flowers along the way.

1*

1

2*

2

1* CARAVAN INTERIORS

Stylist Emily Chalmers is one of the best in the business, and her shop, Caravan Interiors, has long been a go-to for quirky, shabby-chic fans. Vacating her old premises on Shoreditch's Redchurch Street, Emily has downsized to a 'by appointment only' space, in a blink-and-you'll-miss-it unit, down a scruffy side street, underneath a block of flats. But don't let the smaller, less showy premises put you off. This is an Aladdin's cave of Emily's perfectly picked finds. Curtains are fashioned from a patchwork of vintage scarfs, bone china plates are painted with menacing-looking jackdaws, and candles burn in pineapple wall sconces. Make an appointment—who knows what you'll come away with.

5 Ravenscroft Street
E2 7SH
Tel 0207 033 3532
www.caravanstyle.com

2* NELLY DUFF

There's a dark sense of humour running through many works on show in this gallery—like a portrait of Che Guevara fashioned from the logos of US firms that have turned a tidy profit in Cuba. Edgy and just-provocative-enough, the gallery name is emblazoned in bold lights across the shop front, while inside the art hangs on exposed brick walls. All budgets are catered for, with many pieces created exclusively for here. It will be hard to leave empty-handed.

156 Columbia Road
E2 7RG
Tel 0207 033 9683
www.nellyduff.com

3✴ MASON & PAINTER

Homewares designer Michelle Mason already has big retailers—the likes of Liberty, Heal's and House of Fraser—snapping up her distinctive work, but this is the first shop of her very own. And it's gorgeous. Working alongside vintage expert Tim Painter, Michelle has created a wonderland of old and new treasures. Her own iconic London Transport Museum collaborations are here—mugs and cushions stamped with destinations from London's landmark bus routes—but there's so much more. Vintage artworks and glasswear, old pieces of furniture from French flea markets, quirky contemporary designs... If nothing else tempts you, it's hard to resist a Kiss Me Quick tea towel.

136 Columbia Road
E2 7RG
www.masonandpainter.co.uk

4✴ SUCK AND CHEW

Remember the excitement you felt when visiting your local sweet shop as a kid? You can relive it here. This is everything a confectioner's should be, a joyous riot of sugary treats and sticky indulgences. Jars of sweets are measured out by hand into red and white stripy paper bags. Old-fashioned tins are packed with toffees. Retro mugs from the Queen's Coronation and Silver Jubilee are filled to the brim. A handwritten blackboard announces 'salty liquorice is back in'. And to complete the mood, vintage toys, school satchels and Ladybird books are used as decorations, with a string of Union Jack bunting hung over the shop counter. Release your inner child and enjoy.

130 Columbia Road
E2 7RG
0208 983 3504
www.suckandchew.co.uk

5✳ RYANTOWN

Artist Rob Ryan sells his exquisite hand-cut
paper prints around the world, but this is
his only dedicated shop. His studio is just
around the corner, and much of the work
sold here is exclusive. If you don't know his
style, prepare to be enchanted. Whimsical,
romantic and a little bit kooky, his
pictures feature sayings ('Let your heart
have a say', 'I miss being a small girl') that
will have you smiling and feeling fuzzy
around the edges. The shop itself is utterly
charming. With lovely worn floorboards,
hand-stencilled tiles and tea towels
imploring you to 'Believe in People',
it's a world of traditional manners and
romantic daydreams. Just lovely.
126 Columbia Road
E2 7RG
Tel 02076 131 510
www.misterrob.co.uk

6✳ TREACLE

It's hard to think of a better name for a shop that celebrates all things cakey. Reminiscent of postwar London teashops like Lyons and focused on good honest baking, the mood is homely rather than twee—a world away from the too-sugary cake shops that proliferate today. Vintage 1950s kitchen units are stacked high with cooking paraphernalia, everything from collectable old-fashioned tea sets to tea towels and oven gloves. And then there are the cakes themselves, all cooked on the premises. Victoria sponges sit on cake stands ready to be served by the slice, and bite-sized fairy cakes are displayed as iced temptations in an old wooden shop cabinet. Sweet-toothed heaven.

110–112 Columbia Road
E2 7RG
Tel 0207 729 0538

8*

Vintage Heaven

8

7*

7

WOODEN
SPOOL
£.50

7✱ BEYOND FABRICS

If you've never been tempted to take up sewing, you will after a visit here. Acres of vintage-style fabrics and countless haberdashery bits and pieces will bring out your inner cross-stitcher. To say it's a visual feast of colour and pattern doesn't do it justice. Packets of fabric scraps are arranged in a lucky-dip basket, jars of buttons sit on shelves, and a bright-blue brick wall offsets a display of beautiful vintage ribbons. If you're a novice, classes in such skills as quilting and patchwork are on offer in the shop's own work space.

B J House
Unit 2, 10–14 Hollybush Gardens
E2 9QP
Tel 0207 729 5449
www.beyond-fabrics.com

8✱ VINTAGE HEAVEN

There isn't a spare corner left in this shop. Every possible surface is packed with vintage glass, china, cutlery, books, fabrics; if it's from the 1940s to 1960s, chances are you'll find it here. What makes this place extra special is the owner's merchandising eye. There may be mountains of stuff, but it's carefully displayed according to colour, pattern and style. One whole shelf is devoted to glass jelly moulds and butter dishes, another to orange glassware, another to flowery teapots. And on and on it goes. It may be hard to take it all in, but it will be harder to leave without buying at least one thing. If the choice overwhelms you, head out the back to the Cake Hole café. Here, yet more vintage china is not only displayed, but used to serve your tea and cakes. A hoarder's paradise.

82 Columbia Road
E2 7QB
Tel 01277 215 968
www.vintageheaven.co.uk

10*

10*

10*

10*

9✳ CAMPANIA GASTRONOMIA

Prepare to step back in time at this tiny restaurant and café, tucked into a tiny lane off the main Columbia Road drag. The building used to be the milking shed for eight cows, and the bones of the original working dairy are plain to see. These days, it's a temple to great food. The owners are passionate supporters of local suppliers, sourcing as much as they can from fellow foodies in the area. There's a salumi and cheese bar up the front, with aperitifs and wines to wash it all down with. And the wood-fired oven supplies the pizzas, bread and other wood-fired dishes. The cows might not recognise it these days, but their loss is our gain.
23 Ezra Street
E2 7RH
www.columbiaroad.info

10✳ THE LILY VANILLI BAKERY

Some would argue that the world doesn't need another cupcake—but they haven't had a Lily Vanilli cupcake. What began as a Broadway Market stall is now a baking empire that stretches from London to India. The reason for its success is simple: Lily's innovative creations. Her book, *A Zombie Ate My Cupcake*, gives you a clue. Quirky, modern and always delicious, her cakes are never dull. And a Sunday morning apple, thyme and blackberry cupcake is pretty hard to resist. As for the triple-chocolate brownies? They're legendary. Don't be put off by the crowds in this tiny bakery. The wait is worth it.
6 The Courtyard
Ezra Street
E2 7RH
www.lilyvanilli.com/the-bakery

12✱ PRINTERS & STATIONERS

There's something delightfully eccentric about this wine shop and café. Squeezed into a tiny, narrow space, the various alcoholic delights are sold at the front, under antique chandeliers. This place really is all about the drinks. The French owners are big liqueur fans, and there's a tempting line-up of Alice In Wonderland-like bottles on the bar. Order by the glass, or fill your own bottle to take away. The menu is limited to one dish per night if you're dining in the tiny one-table room out the back, and a small selection of sandwiches and pastries to take away. There's a record player and vinyl selection for customers to play their own tunes, and one of the co-owners even offers 'soul plan' readings—similar to numerology apparently... Truly a one-off kind of place.
21a Ezra Street
E2 7RH
www.printersandstationers.co.uk

13✱ BRAWN

Impeccable food in a laid-back and East-London groovy setting make Brawn a must-stop eating spot. Sit at one of the old school tables and chairs and order from a menu packed with meaty treats—as the name suggests, this isn't a particularly vegetarian-friendly place. With cool art on the walls, a rough concrete floor and staff who seem more like helpful friends than paid professionals, it's the perfect place for a very long lunch.
49 Columbia Road
E2 7RG
Tel 0207 729 5692
www.brawn.co

michael & charlotte sager-wilde

What started as a once-a-week pop-up is now one of the hippest drinking joints in London. Sager + Wilde is the creation of husband-and-wife wine experts Michael and Charlotte Sager-Wilde. It began life as a Thursday evening wine night in nearby Old Street, but their handpicked wines proved so popular that they took over a tiny Victorian pub and opened full time. With a mood that mixes old-world charm (parquet floors, exposed brickwork, silver candlesticks) with East London industrial chic (architectural salvage lighting, cast-iron bar top), the squeezy space is always packed. London's coolest wine bar.

Sager + Wilde
193 Hackney Road E2 8JL ✤ **www.sagerandwilde.com**

'When a man is tired of London, he is tired of life'

How would you define London style?

Dr Johnson, the English literary giant, said of London, 'When a man is tired of London, he is tired of life'. London is made up of small villages, each with their individual style. Collectively it's a mash-up of timeless panache, based on historical antecedents, combined with the energetic bravura of emerging new talent.

Where do you go to be inspired?

We love Chiswick and Battersea car boot sales (www.batterseaboot.com, www.chiswickcarbootsale.com), charity shops and Kempton Park antiques (www.sunburyantiques.com) just outside of London. We also love **Retrouvious** (see page 190) and The Architectural Forum (www.thearchitecturalforum.com), both very talented salvage professionals.

Your favourite local places?

The Quality Chop House (see page 86), St. John Bread & Wine (www. stjohnbreadandwine.com) and Rochelle Canteen (www.arnoldandhenderson. com).

115

What's in your secret shopping address book?

Noble Fine Liquor (www.noblefineliquor.co.uk) on Broadway Market has a great beer selection and interesting wines, and Androuet (www.androuet.co.uk) in Spitalfields is best for cheese. YMC (www.youmustcreate.com) in Spitalfields is great for clothing, as is **Hostem** on Redchurch Street (see page 157).

Describe your perfect out-and-about weekend?

On Saturdays we go to The Hops & Glory pub on Essex Road (www.hopsandglory.co.uk) for amazing beers. Then, a matinee at Screen On The Green (www.everymancinema.com). Just further down from the cinema there's some really lovely antique shops on Chapel Market. Street Feast (www.streetfeastlondon.com) and Hawker House night markets are brilliant in the evening. We live just behind Columbia Road, so normally grab coffee and flowers at the flower market on Sundays before heading into work just after lunch time. Lunch at **Brawn** on Columbia Road is lovely too (see page 113).

Best place for a weekend supper?

The **Clove Club** (see page 163) and **Brunswick House Café** (see page 289) are both consistently brilliant.

Best place for a drink?

Satan's Whiskers (see page 176) on Cambridge Heath Road; it only plays hip hop and R&B and their drinks are killer. And Happiness Forgets on Hoxton Square (www.happinessforgets.com).

Your favourite breakfast spot?

Rita's Bar & Dining in Hackney for brunch (ritasbaranddining.com).

Where do you go to relax?

Regent's Canal. It runs all the way through Islington and Dalston, up to Broadway Market and Hackney Wick. It's a really interesting walk. The moored barges are awesome, and the surrounding architecture is so diverse, from Victorian cottages and warehouses, to factories from a bygone age. There's a really peaceful part in Hackney Wick where you can walk off the path and go to the more newly developed area that has a great Brewery called CRATE (www.cratebrewery.com). And there's a fab café restaurant called The Hackney Pearl (www.thehackneypearl.com). Just before that there's **Broadway Market** (see page 118), which is brilliant on Saturday mornings for the food and clothing stalls.

Favourite cultural sights?

The Whitechapel Gallery (www.whitechapelgallery.org), because it's an institution in East London. A proper East End gallery in a great location, with great history, architecture, and exceptionally well curated exhibits. And the V&A (www.vam.ac.uk), because of the calibre of the exhibitions that have an intense focus on art and design—but predominantly for their spectacular fashion retrospectives. And the gift shop always has amazing cards.

Top three things that every visitor to London should do?

Go to Sager + Wilde wine bar on Hackney Road. We hear it's awesome! Go for coffee and casual market food at Borough Market (www.boroughmarket.org.uk) on Saturday morning. Also **Maltby Street market** (see page 50) on Saturday morning. Lunch at **40 Maltby Street** (see page 61) is always mega. Then walk all the way along the river to Tate Modern (www.tate.org.uk) and go for a glass of wine at the bar on the fourth floor. It has a spectacular view of St Paul's Cathedral and the surrounding area.

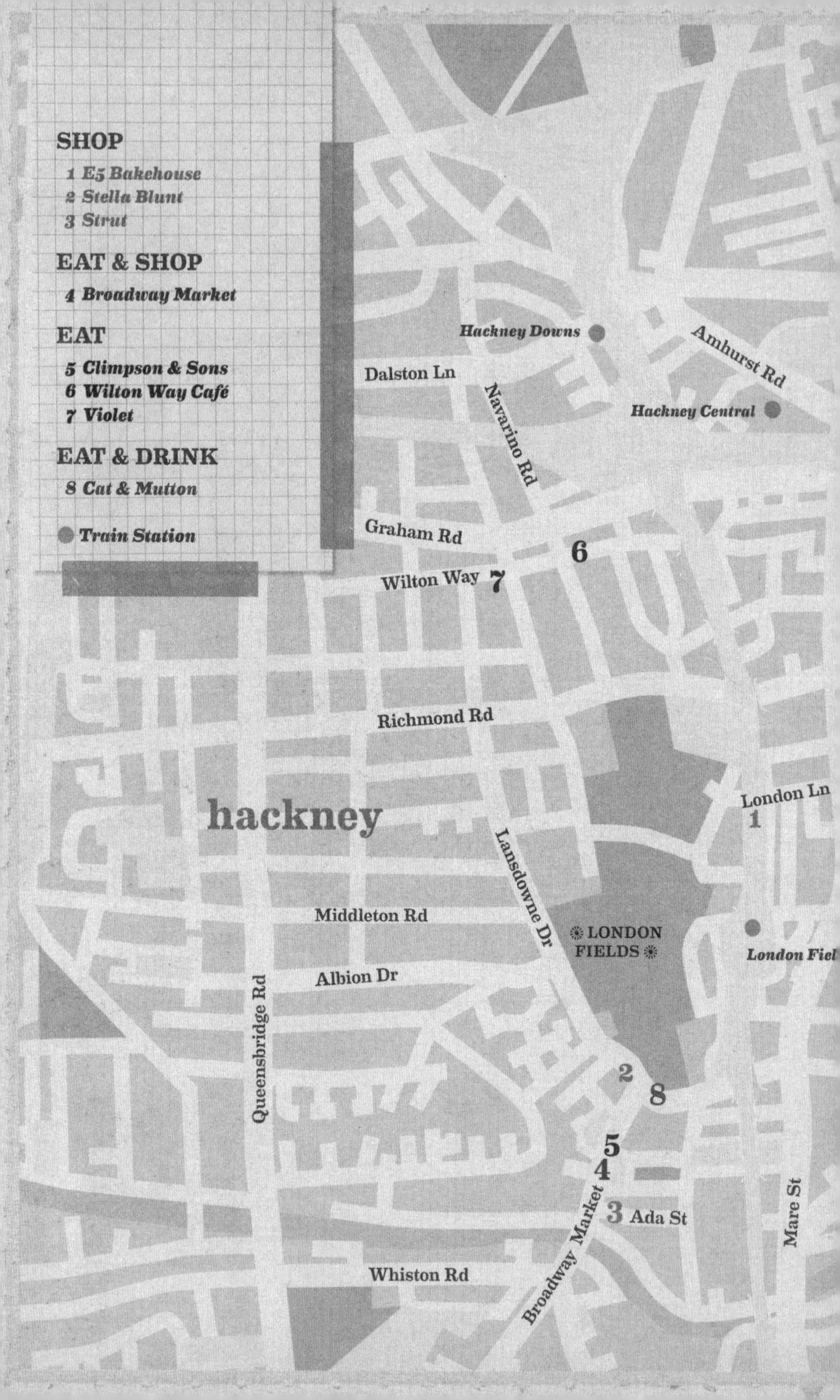

Hackney Downs ●

Amhurst Rd

Dalston Ln

Navarino Rd

Hackney Central ●

Graham Rd

Wilton Way 7

6

Richmond Rd

hackney

London Ln

1

Lansdowne Dr

Middleton Rd

Albion Dr

Queensbridge Rd

⊛ LONDON
FIELDS ⊛

London Fiel●

2

8

5

4

3 Ada St

Broadway Market

Mare St

Whiston Rd

london fields

A Saturday outing to Broadway Market in London Fields, Hackney, is a must. As soon as you arrive, you'll notice that it's a seriously trendy hangout—coffee-sipping bright young things spill out of cafés onto the pavement, congregate in the pubs and stroll up and down the market's food and vintage clothes stalls. If you love a bit of people watching, you've come to the right place. But it's not just the market stalls that are worth a visit. The area around the green expanse of London Fields has a wealth of independent outlets, tucked into railway arches and hidden among the surrounding residential streets. No wonder it's one of the city's hippest addresses. Come and join the fun.

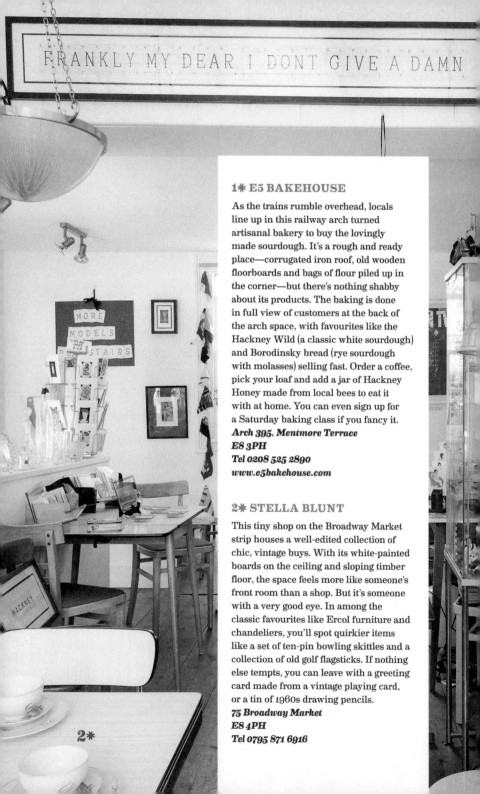

1✸ E5 BAKEHOUSE

As the trains rumble overhead, locals line up in this railway arch turned artisanal bakery to buy the lovingly made sourdough. It's a rough and ready place—corrugated iron roof, old wooden floorboards and bags of flour piled up in the corner—but there's nothing shabby about its products. The baking is done in full view of customers at the back of the arch space, with favourites like the Hackney Wild (a classic white sourdough) and Borodinsky bread (rye sourdough with molasses) selling fast. Order a coffee, pick your loaf and add a jar of Hackney Honey made from local bees to eat it with at home. You can even sign up for a Saturday baking class if you fancy it.
Arch 395, Mentmore Terrace
E8 3PH
Tel 0208 525 2890
www.e5bakehouse.com

2✸ STELLA BLUNT

This tiny shop on the Broadway Market strip houses a well-edited collection of chic, vintage buys. With its white-painted boards on the ceiling and sloping timber floor, the space feels more like someone's front room than a shop. But it's someone with a very good eye. In among the classic favourites like Ercol furniture and chandeliers, you'll spot quirkier items like a set of ten-pin bowling skittles and a collection of old golf flagsticks. If nothing else tempts, you can leave with a greeting card made from a vintage playing card, or a tin of 1960s drawing pencils.
75 Broadway Market
E8 4PH
Tel 0795 871 6916

3✱ STRUT

A far cry from the usual slightly fusty, vintage clothing store, Strut is about as urban and modern-looking as it gets. With a polished concrete floor, exposed ceiling surfaces and painted breeze-block walls, everything about it says 21st century. The only clue to its vintage soul is the original shop fittings from Mary Quant's 1960s London store. The clothes are a mix of high-class vintage (think a full-length Ossie Clark crepe dress, a Biba shirt and Gucci suitcase), hardly worn designer second hand (the likes of Stella McCartney and Martin Margiela), and a few new pieces from top-end names such as Balenciaga. It's a tempting mix.

2B Ada Street
E8 4QU
Tel 0207 254 8121
www.strutlondon.com

123

4✳ BROADWAY MARKET

On Saturdays, Broadway Market comes alive with stalls selling everything from organic meat and cheese to kids' clothing and bric-a-brac. There's even a hog spit roast. Grab a takeaway coffee from **Climpson & Sons** (see page 126) and go for a wander. Here are a few favourites to look out for.

Drake & Naylor: Fun, affordable and useful vintage design from the 1950s to 1980s. If your home needs an angle poise lamp, a piece of taxidermy or set of 1970s brass swallows, you'll find it here. www.drakeandnaylor.co.uk

Sue Goodman: Remember the Ladybird and I-Spy books of your childhood? Sue has stockpiled them. It will all come flooding back as you look through the titles. Half the fun is listening to fellow customers gasp as they spot the book that their eight-year-old-self loved.

Alice Gabb: There's something quintessentially British and quirky about turning a vintage royal commemorative mug into a candle. And that's what Alice does. A 1902 King Edward VII and Queen Alexandra coronation mug is filled with eco soy wax. Ditto a Queen Elizabeth II Silver Jubilee mug. There's even Charles and Diana wedding china ready to burn. Lovely souvenirs for anyone after an unusual bit of Britishness.

CLIMPSON & SONS MENU

- Granola, yoghurt and fresh berries £3.50
- Bircher muesli, yoghurt pistachios & honey £3.50
- Toast with choice of spreads £1.50
- Crumpets with choice of spreads £1.80

✳ Gluten free bread available.

- Chickpea & artichoke salad with grilled halloumi £5.00
- Chicken, avocado, feta and pine nuts with honey mustard dressing £5.00
- Smoked mackerel, beetroot & horseradish £5.00

- Avocado & tomato salsa on sourdough toast £2.50
  – add smoked salmon +£2.50
- Grilled halloumi & houmous sandwich £3.90
- Gourmet pies, with pea, feta & mint salad £5.50

✳ Ask staff for details

5 ✳ CLIMPSON & SONS

The spot on Broadway Market where the cool kids hang, this coffee shop is never not packed, with locals crammed into every corner and spilling out onto the pavement benches. It's all about the coffee, hand-roasted at the café's nearby roastery. It helps too, that the place looks effortlessly hip. The lovely old shop front and funky interior are a winning combination—try to find yourself a spot, if you can. For those who can't squeeze in, there's always the online coffee-selling service. Not quite the same as experiencing an espresso and a snack in person, though.

67 Broadway Market
E8 4PH
Tel 0207 812 9829
www.climpsonandsons.com

London Fields Ra

6✳ WILTON WAY CAFÉ

How many cafés have a DJ booth from
which the local community radio station
broadcasts? This is that kind of place,
but you need to know about it to find it.
Away from the main Broadway Market
drag, it's tucked away down a picturesque
residential side street. If only there was
a café like this in every neighbourhood.
The food and coffee are delicious, and
it's a joy just to sit here soaking up the
neighbourhood vibe. Reclaimed materials
such as corrugated iron and old pieces of
wood create a laid-back feel, there's local
artists' works on the walls and the staff
are smiling. Get your timing right and
visit the weekend of the Wilton Way
street fair, and you'll find the café at the
heart of it all, with a pop-up bookshop
inside, vintage vans on the street outside
and even a dog show.

63 Wilton Way
E8 1BG
Tel 0779 375 4776

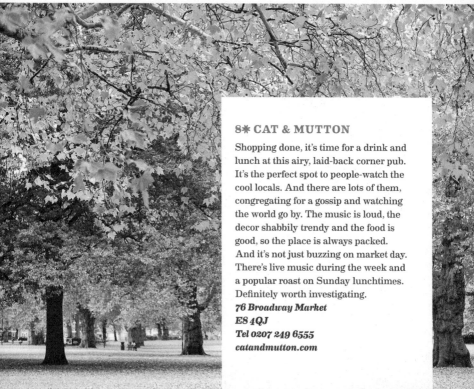

8 ✳ CAT & MUTTON

Shopping done, it's time for a drink and lunch at this airy, laid-back corner pub. It's the perfect spot to people-watch the cool locals. And there are lots of them, congregating for a gossip and watching the world go by. The music is loud, the decor shabbily trendy and the food is good, so the place is always packed. And it's not just buzzing on market day. There's live music during the week and a popular roast on Sunday lunchtimes. Definitely worth investigating.

76 Broadway Market
E8 4QJ
Tel 0207 249 6555
catandmutton.com

The Cat & Mutton

Lunch 12-3

- Tomato & Basil Soup & Bread £5
- Pork Belly Sandwich w/ Apple Sauce & Rocket £6
- Sardines on Toast w/ Capers & Chilli Butter £8
- Deep Fried Sprats w/ Smoked Paprika Mayo & Brown Bread £6
- Pan Fried Halloumi w/ Apple, Pecan & Beetroot Dressing £7.50
- Linguine w/ Stem Broccoli Cashel Blue Sauce & Crispy Bread crumbs £9.50
- Homemade Burger w/ Cheddar, Dijon Chutney, Coleslaw & Chips £10
- Wild Boar & Chorizo Sausages, Mash Potato, Green Beans & Gravy £9.50
- Smoked Black Pudding, Bacon, Potato & Rocket Salad w/ Poached Egg £8
- Salmon & Herring Fishcake w/ Fennel Tomato, Rocket & Tartare Sauce £8.50
- Devilled Lamb Kidneys w/ Bubble & Squeak £8
- Chicken Schnitzel w/ Warm Onion & Potato Salad, Cucumber & Mint Yoghurt £9.50

- Apple & Plum Crumble w/ Crème Anglaise £5
- Sticky Toffee Pudding w/ Vanilla Ice Cream £5
- Selection of Ice Cream: Cherry, Salt Caramel, Rhubarb, Vanilla, Raspberry, Banana - 2 scoops = £4 / 3 scoops = £5.50
- Selection of Neal's Yard Cheeses w/ Homemade Chutney & Oat Cakes £9.50
  (Keen's Cheddar, Cashel Blue, Stawley Goats & St James' soft)

claire ptak

It may be small, but this cake shop and café packs a punch. Violet began and still trades at Saturday's Broadway Market, but operates throughout the week at this bricks-and-mortar venue on Wilton Way. It's a mecca for sweet-toothed aficionados who travel across London for its famous cupcakes—and a lot more besides. Owner and Hackney resident Claire Ptak worked as a pastry chef at the legendary Chez Panisse in Berkeley, California, and from the moment you see the blackboard outside announcing specials like Salted Caramel Whoopie Pies, you know you're dealing with a cake creator at the top of her game. No wonder there's always a queue. Treat yourself to a slice of ginger molasses cake to take home, or sit in and enjoy the atmosphere.

VIOLET
47 Wilton Way E8 3ED ❖ 0207 275 8360 ❖ www.violetcakes.com

'I love to sit in the Rose Bakery on top of Dover Street Market overlooking the rooftops in Piccadilly'

How would you define London style?

Coming from California where everyone has a car, I am always impressed by London women cycling and taking the Tube in awesome shoes (often heels). London girls really wear their shoes into the ground and I love that!

Where do you go in London to be inspired?

I get a lot of inspiration standing behind my stall at Broadway Market. Everyone looks amazing. I also love to sit in the Rose Bakery on top of **Dover Street Market** (see page 282) and drink tea from their lovely pots overlooking the rooftops in Piccadilly.

Your favourite local places?

I love to walk up to Dalston to eat at the Mangal Turkish Pizza (27 Stoke Newington Road, N16 8BJ, tel 0207 254 6999), and then go see a film at the Rio Cinema (www.riocinema.org.uk). I also love the Railroad café on Morning Lane (www. railroadhackney.co.uk), run by boyfriend and girlfriend Lizzy and Matt. They cook from their hearts. Of course **Towpath Café** (see page 142) is a favourite, too. My friends

Lori and Jason started it around the same time I opened my shop. It's nice to see your friends do well in similar businesses.

What's in your secret shopping address book?

I love a little shop called Egg on Kinnerton Street (www.eggtrading.com) in West London. They have the most amazing scarves and aprons. I also love jewellery and three of my favourite designers are from London. Natasha Collis (www.natashacollis.com) for her rough-cut stones and gold nuggets, Katie Hillier (www.hillierlondon.com) for her animal paperclip necklaces, and Pippa Small (www.pippasmall.com) for her wonderful use of natural pearls.

Where's the best place for a weekend supper?

I am a huge fan of the River Café (www.rivercafe.co.uk). I am never disappointed and I love the room.

Best place for a drink?

I love to get a drink in the dizzying viewing gallery on the 33rd floor at Paramount (www.paramount.uk.net), in the Centre Point building on Tottenham Court Road. There is a 360-degree view of London and it reminds me where I am.

Where do you go in London to relax?

I feel very relaxed walking through the beautiful fern groves in the Epping Forest (www.eppingforestdc.gov.uk), where my husband and I take our dog Shuggie some Sundays. It is slightly outside London, but I still think it counts.

Favourite cultural sights?

Dennis Severs' House in Spitalfields (www.dennissevershouse.co.uk). It is especially magical in the winter when it is dark so early. I also love to go to Tate Britain (www.tate.org.uk) and then take the shuttle boat to the Tate Modern. But I don't spend too long at each place. Art gallery overkill is a bad thing.

'I am always impressed by London women cycling and taking the Tube in awesome shoes'

135

SHOP

1 Pictures & Light
2 LN-CC
3 Pelicans & Parrots

EAT & DRINK

4 Sutton & Sons
5 Dalston Roof Park
6 Dalston Eastern
   Curve Garden
7 Towpath Café
8 Jones & Sons

● Train Station

1

Stoke Newington Church St

Stoke Newington High St

4

● Rectory Road

❋ HACKNEY
DOWNS ❋

3

8

Arcola St

Shackwell Ln

**stoke
newington**

2

dalston

Sandringham Rd

Kingsland High St

● Dalston Kingsland

Ashwin St

5   6

Balls Pond Rd

● Dalston Ln

Dalston Junction

De Beauvoir Rd

● Haggerston

Kingsland Rd

Downham Rd

Whitmore Bridge

7

Grand Union Canal

stoke newington & dalston

It's hard to imagine a better example of London as a city of contrasts. From the village-like streets of Stoke Newington, it's a short stroll to the gritty urban vibe of Dalston. Although neighbours geographically, the two locales couldn't be more different, and the contrast is fascinating. Stroll along the leafy loveliness of Stoke Newington Church Street, then turn into Stoke Newington High Street and enter a different zone. While Stoke Newington is a pocket of slow-paced, genteel London life, Dalston is where the younger, cooler crowd are congregating. Watching the two worlds collide is what makes London such an endlessly fascinating place to be.

1✸ PICTURES & LIGHT

Owner Justine Blair has a brilliant eye
for style, and her shop reflects her love
of both vintage and new design. The walls
are hung with a mass of vintage mirrors
and the shelves lined with old pottery
and coloured glassware. A cabinet shelf
of delicately coloured buttons looks like
a tray of sweets. Local artists' prints have
pride of place alongside vintage Cuban
film posters, while one-off touches of
madness, like a turn-of-the-century string
dispenser fashioned as a woman's head
(the string comes out through her mouth),
add the odd element of surprise.
41 Stoke Newington Church Street
N16 0NX
Tel 0207 923 7923

2✸ LN-CC

Possibly the winner of 'London's most
hidden shop' award, the by-appointment-
only Late Night Chameleon Café (to
give it its full title) is a luxury fashion
empire disguised as a disused basement
warehouse. For a start, there's no shop
sign. Come down an alleyway, ring the
buzzer and only then do you realise
what's been created in this former boxing
gym. Quite literally, a whole new world.
More like a stage set than a shop interior,
you enter through a corridor of trees—
the 'forest'—and then walk through
another tunnel of plywood and Perspex
panels. The effect is surreal. The clothes
themselves, when you get to them, are
high end, a mix of upcoming designers
and established labels. But even if you
don't buy a thing, it's worth visiting for
the experience. There's also a bookshop
and club space (used for private events).
No wonder the likes of Coldplay and
Kanye West are customers—no one
would know they were here.
18–24 Shacklewell Lane
E8 2EZ
Tel 0207 275 7265
www.ln-cc.com

VIVA LA D.R.P!

5*

4*

4* SUTTON & SONS

Forget images of a greasy local chippie. This is funky fish and chips. The decor is stripped-wood communal benches, chic industrial light fittings, cool black and white tiling on the walls, and a stylish line-drawn mural of local scenes running the length of the room. As for the food, how about the catch of the day, grilled British sea bass? Or grilled line-caught mackerel? The local chippie reinvented.

90 Stoke Newington High Street
N16 7NY
Tel 0207 249 6444
www.suttonandsons.co.uk

5* DALSTON ROOF PARK

Climb the 60-plus stairs of this Victorian building (a warning: there's no lift), and you come out onto an unexpected green space. Okay, it's AstroTurf, not grass—but with raised beds growing flowers, tomatoes, strawberries, lettuce and other assorted veg, it's not what you'd imagine in the heart of the East End. The rooftop bar is open seasonally (check the website for details), hosting film nights, live DJs and other local events. Even better, the whole enterprise is run as a charity, with money raised going to local community projects. But just come for the views—sipping a drink as you gaze out over the cityscape makes it well worth the climb.

The Print House
18 Ashwin Street
E8 3DL
www.bootstrapcompany.co.uk

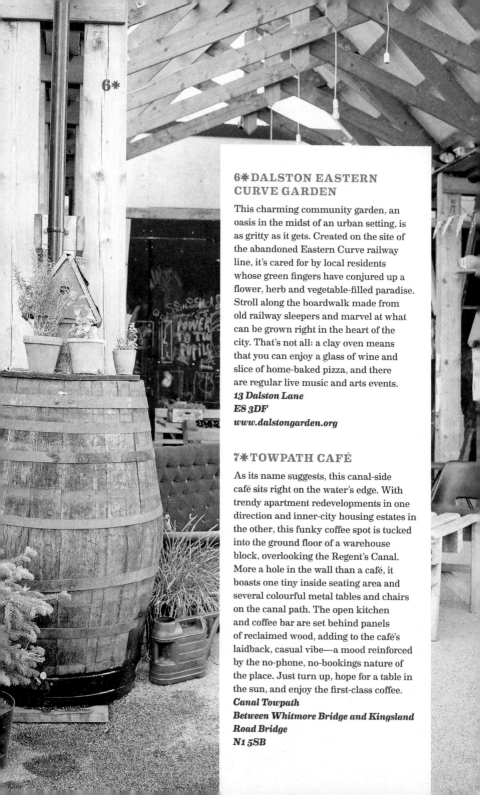

6*DALSTON EASTERN CURVE GARDEN

This charming community garden, an oasis in the midst of an urban setting, is as gritty as it gets. Created on the site of the abandoned Eastern Curve railway line, it's cared for by local residents whose green fingers have conjured up a flower, herb and vegetable-filled paradise. Stroll along the boardwalk made from old railway sleepers and marvel at what can be grown right in the heart of the city. That's not all: a clay oven means that you can enjoy a glass of wine and slice of home-baked pizza, and there are regular live music and arts events.

13 Dalston Lane
E8 3DF
www.dalstongarden.org

7*TOWPATH CAFÉ

As its name suggests, this canal-side café sits right on the water's edge. With trendy apartment redevelopments in one direction and inner-city housing estates in the other, this funky coffee spot is tucked into the ground floor of a warehouse block, overlooking the Regent's Canal. More a hole in the wall than a café, it boasts one tiny inside seating area and several colourful metal tables and chairs on the canal path. The open kitchen and coffee bar are set behind panels of reclaimed wood, adding to the café's laidback, casual vibe—a mood reinforced by the no-phone, no-bookings nature of the place. Just turn up, hope for a table in the sun, and enjoy the first-class coffee.

Canal Towpath
Between Whitmore Bridge and Kingsland Road Bridge
N1 5SB

7*

8* JONES & SONS

This classic British restaurant and café
is refreshingly understated—hip, but
in a quietly grown-up way. Formerly
a Victorian-era textile factory, it takes
its style cues from Danish design and
industrial luxe, with a concrete floor,
exposed brickwork and lights sourced
from a marine salvage specialist in
Exeter. But it's the food that truly steals
the show. From classics with a twist
(sticky toffee pudding with ginger ice
cream) to old-fashioned favourites (game
pie and venison haunch), the traditional
British menu is a crowd pleaser. As are
the warm and welcoming staff, with
their East London regulation beards
and friendly smiles. Whether you want
to soothe a sore head with a Bloody Mary
over brunch, or stretch out a Sunday
afternoon with a sirloin roast, this is a
place you won't want to leave in a hurry.
23–27 Arcola Street
E8 2DJ
0207 241 1211
www.jonesandsonsdalston.com

8*

143

juliet da silva

Along with co-owner Ochuko Ojiri, Juliet da Silva has created a quirkily chic vintage haven on this scruffy-but-cool stretch of East London high street. With Dalston rapidly turning itself into the go-to zone for London's hip young things, it's no surprise that Pelicans & Parrots is top of the list for interiors stylists and anyone who loves a well-chosen retro buy. For the home, you'll find Victorian curiosities, old prints, antlers, glass pharmacy jars, even a stuffed peacock. And for your wardrobe there's a well-edited selection of vintage fashion finds. Juliet also throws some contemporary buys into the mix—like Abigail Ahern's kooky lamp bases (see page 32)—so that the whole effect is modern rather than dated. Expect some surprises, too. A vivid red-feathered Notting Hill carnival headdress isn't one for shrinking violets.

PELICANS & PARROTS
40 Stoke Newington Road N16 7XJ ❧ 0203 215 2083 ❧ www.pelicansandparrots.com

'Various carnival bands put on club nights all around London'

How would you define London style?
Effortless elegance.

Where do you go in London to be inspired?
The Thursday antiques market in Spitalfields (www.oldspitalfieldsmarket.com). It's great for unusual objects and colourful characters.

Your favourite local places?
Ridley Road Market has a great Trinidadian roti stall at weekends.

Describe your perfect out-and-about weekend?
People-watching in London Fields Hackney, cocktails, then on to a good Soca night for a dance. Various carnival bands put on club nights all around London.

What's in your secret shopping address book?
Mawi on Calvert Avenue in Shoreditch (www.mawi.co.uk). It's a piece of West End luxury hidden in the east. Great for a window shop.

145

Where's the best place for a weekend supper?

Canteen in Spitalfields (www.canteen. co.uk). It's classic British food: local and informal.

Best place for a drink?

Bardens Boudoir next to our shop in Dalston (www.bardensboudoir. co.uk). It's so easy, down-to-earth and reasonably priced. Plus, it's right next door!

Your favourite breakfast spot?

Shoreditch House (see page 165) is a nice start to the day, and the views from the rooftop are great.

Favourite cultural sights?

I like Trellick Tower in West London, and I never tire of the view as you drive over Tower Bridge.

Top three things that every visitor to London should do?

Visit Notting Hill Carnival on August bank holiday weekend, preferably in a carnival costume. Go to a car boot sale; it's a good way to meet the real locals of any area. Princess May in Dalston is excellent (www.thelondoncarbootco. co.uk). And have a coffee in Allpress on Redchurch Street (58 Redchurch Street, E2 7DP, tel 0207 749 1780). Delicious.

SHOP

1 Present
2 Labour and Wait
3 Celestine Eleven
4 Blitz
5 Tatty Devine
6 Hostem
7 Le Grenier
8 Start London

EAT & DRINK

9 The Book Club
10 The Owl & Pussycat
11 Pizza East
12 Albion
13 The Clove Club
14 Story Deli

EAT, DRINK, SLEEP (& SWIM!)

15 Shoreditch House

SLEEP

16 Ace Hotel
17 40 Winks

● Tube Station
● Train Station

Hoxton

bethnal green

Calvert Ave

13
8

5

16
1
12
6
2
14
7
10 Redchurch St
Bethnal Green Rd

3

11 15
Cheshire St

Shoreditch High Street

Tabernacle St
Paul St
Leonard St 9
Great Eastern St

shoreditch

Shoreditch High St

Brick Lane

Hanbury St 4

17

Liverpool Street

shoreditch

If there's a hipper area in town right now, I'm struggling to think of it. Dalston may have the up-and-coming edge, but Shoreditch is still the place where hordes of skinny-jeaned trendies flock. It's got it all. Cool, independent shops and cafés, markets, chic interiors boutiques, edgy record shops, grungy vintage emporiums and a hefty dose of gritty urban style. On weekends, expect crowds and world-class people watching. Go for a wander, and if you can swing it, end the day on the rooftop of Shoreditch House private member's club—the best spot in town to survey the scene.

1✳ PRESENT

This cult menswear store is a mecca for men who want to look fashionable but not too trend-led. Shopping starts with a coffee, made by the in-store barista—how many clothes shops offer that? It pretty much sets the tone: unexpected, hip and a bit quirky. The shop itself, with its original Golden Horn Cigarette Company frontage, is a sleek industrial-like space, complete with polished concrete floor and effortlessly cool shop assistants (all unfailingly friendly). Alongside the clothes—a perfectly curated mix of labels, with a focus on styles with heritage and a bit of a twist—are accessories, design books, magazines and the odd candle or two. And if you're really stuck, an Uzi Submachine Gun Paper Model Kit or a bottle of Aēsop animal shampoo should do the trick.

140 Shoreditch High Street
E1 6JE
Tel 0207 033 0500
www.present-london.com

2✳ LABOUR AND WAIT

Who'd have thought a shop that describes its stock as 'traditional products for the home' could be so stylish. This is no dingy corner hardware store, but an institution famous for its meticulously presented range of basic household wares. Classic utilitarian objects are celebrated as things of style. There's no plastic tat, just beautifully made wood and metal goods; when even a container of rubber hot water bottles looks elegant, it's testament to how brilliantly put together the whole place is. You will leave with a giant ball of string you never knew you wanted—but which you will cherish.
85 Redchurch Street
E2 7DJ
Tel 0207 729 6253
www.labourandwait.co.uk

3✳ CELESTINE ELEVEN

There aren't many places where you'll find a secret yoga club downstairs (www.secretyogaclub.co.uk), and designer clothing upstairs. But this is an unusual enterprise. Scratch the sleek designer surface and you'll discover that it also hires out treatment rooms in the basement to alternative therapists. It's an unorthodox blend of different worlds, but it works. The laid-back, openness of the friendly staff belies the upscale nature of the products they sell: some of the coolest names in men's and women's fashion, from J.W. Anderson to Meadham Kirchhoff to Hussein Chalayan. There's a sprinkling of homewares too, such as organic linens and Japanese beauty curios.
4 Holywell Lane
EC2A 3ET
Tel 0207 729 2987
www.celestineeleven.com

5*

5*

4* BLITZ

If you think you're not a fan of vintage clothing, this place will change your mind. On the scale of a department store, the vast space is an old furniture factory that has been transformed into a destination in its own right. There are clothes, of course— nothing shoddy, just rails and rails of handpicked, beautifully presented styles, most of which barely look worn—but there's also antique furniture, records and books, complete with squashy leather sofas to read them in. Oh, and a coffee bar. With its exposed brick walls, old wood floors and chandeliers hanging from the cavernous ceilings, this is vintage with polish.

55–59 Hanbury Street
E1 5JP
Tel 0207 377 0730
www.blitzlondon.co.uk

5* TATTY DEVINE

This cult London jewellery label is loved for its cheeky, quirky Perspex jewellery, all of it made within a short walk of the shop. A very British sense of humour shines through, as in a giant lobster necklace, or an Inspector Clouseau-like moustache hanging on a chain. Their bright custom-made name necklaces are big sellers—even model Claudia Schiffer has one. Pop in. The collection is guaranteed to make you smile.

236 Brick Lane
E2 7EB
Tel 0207 739 9191
www.tattydevine.com

6*

6*

7*

7*

6✴ HOSTEM

Fashion is serious business at Hostem. The ground-floor menswear shop may look bijou, but head up the narrow staircase and the space opens up into a cavernous temple of high-end designer style. Let's be clear, shopping like this does not come cheap. The creations of some of the biggest names hang like works of art on copper coat hangers. Rick Owens, Commes des Garçons, Yohji Yamamoto (£75 leopard print socks, anyone?)—all the serious influencers are here, plus up-and-coming British labels. If money is no object, the leather handbags from Delvaux will make a serious dent. Hostem is one of just a few stockists of Delvaux in the UK, which gives you an idea of the calibre of the merchandise here. That said, the utterly charming staff will welcome you for an 'if only' browse. They seem to be as excited working in this gorgeous space as the rest of us are retail day-dreaming in it.
41–43 Redchurch Street
E2 7DJ
Tel 0207 739 9733
www.hostem.co.uk

7✴ LE GRENIER

As befits its name—*le grenier* is French for 'the attic'—this tiny shop is packed with vintage curiosities. At first glance, the amount of stock is overwhelming, with every surface covered in stacks of china, glassware, quirky objects, jewellery and other bits and pieces. There's a lot to take in. But there are treasures to be found. An elegant Ercol chair sits alongside vintage German school science charts; 1950s Formica kitchen units stand beneath an antique chandelier. Have a rummage and you're guaranteed to unearth something you like.
146 Bethnal Green Road
E2 6DG
Tel 0207 790 7379
le-grenier.com

9*

10

9*

9*

9*

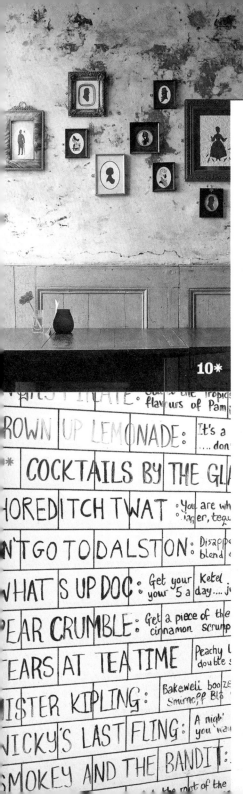

9✳ THE BOOK CLUB

Think of the coolest student common room you never had, filled with the hippest kids in the class, and that's The Book Club. An all-day, all-night venue, it's one big space of exposed brickwork, industrial lights and quirky art on the walls. Off to the side, a table tennis room is packed with bright young things engaged in a King Pong tournament. But it's not just an eating and drinking spot. As well as live music and DJs, you can pop along for an evening life drawing class, a lecture on contemporary design or a spot of speed dating. Definitely one of the local hot spots.

100 Leonard Street
EC2A 4RH
Tel 0207 684 8618
www.wearetbc.com

10✳ THE OWL & PUSSYCAT

This dark and den-like pub is a local favourite. Housed in a late 17th-century Grade II listed building, it has kept all the original features (with some 19th-century additions) and added a cool East End twist. The low ceilings and sloping wooden floors are all intact, but look carefully at the wallpaper, and you'll see that it's actually images of tall ships printed onto a denim-like fabric. Victorian cameo silhouette prints hang on one wall, modern art on another. The mix of historic (the pub stands on the edge of what was one of the worst 19th-century slums) and modern day gives the place a unique charm. Plus the fact that it's one of the best Sunday lunch spots in the area— the traditional roast is a winner. London heritage brought up to date.

34 Redchurch Street
E2 7DP
Tel 0203 487 0088
owlandpussycatshoreditch.com

11✳ PIZZA EAST

London's hippest pizzeria. Owned by the creators of Soho House (their Shoreditch venture is upstairs in the same vast warehouse building, see page 165), this feels more like a club than a restaurant—loud music, stripped-back industrial chic decor and lots of beautiful people. The food is, quite simply, delicious. Start with the likes of fig, burrata and honeycomb bruschetta, and then try to decide on just one choice from the pizza menu. One visit is not going to be enough.

56 Shoreditch High Street
E1 6JJ
Tel 0207 729 1888
www.pizzaeast.com

12✳ ALBION

This street-level café and bakery, on the ground floor of the Boundary hotel, is the perfect brunch spot. A light, airy space with big doors opening onto the cobbled street, it's buzzy and crowded from 8 am to 11 pm. Specialising in traditional British fare, breakfast is particularly good, but a late-night Welsh rarebit or beef and stout pie is pretty hard to beat. As you'd expect from a place created by British design legend Sir Terence Conran, Albion is a beautifully designed room, with old wooden floors, funky industrial fittings and a mix of small and communal tables. And that Conran eye for quirky-but-cool detail is everywhere. Old tins of Lyle's Golden Syrup are used to store vintage-style cutlery, and bottles of Heinz tomato sauce and HP brown sauce have pride of place on the tables. Don't miss the shop, filled with goodies from the bakery and wooden trays of organic veg from Conran's own kitchen garden.

2–4 Boundary Street
E2 7DD
0207 729 1051
www.albioncaff.co.uk

13*

THE CLOVE CLUB

13*

14*

14*

13✳ THE CLOVE CLUB

When is a pop-up not a pop-up? When it takes over the ground floor of a Victorian council building and turns itself into one of London's most bookable dining spaces. The 19th-century, Grade II heritage-listed Shoreditch Town Hall is now permanent home to The Clove Club, run by a team of chefs who made their name with supper clubs in Dalston and a pub restaurant in Spitalfields. The space itself still feels undeniably municipal, pared back to the point of plain. If you want your dining experience accompanied by plush upholstery, crisp tablecloths and a Michelin star, then this is not for you. If, however, you appreciate out-of-this-world cooking, presented without formalities or fancy cushioned seats, then you'll love it here. And the food really is good. Lunchtime offers a set tasting menu only, with boldly flavoured dishes like roast scallop, chervil, seaweed oil and miyagawa satsuma. By night, there's the choice of the set menu or à la carte. (The buttermilk fried chicken is legendary.) And don't miss a peek at the Salumi Room, where all the restaurant's cured meats are aged.

Shoreditch Town Hall
380 Old Street
EC1V 9LT
Tel 0207 729 6496
www.thecloveclub.com

14✳ STORY DELI

Sometimes you come across a place that is so perfect, you're tempted to keep it to yourself. This is one such place. To call it a pizzeria is to wildly undersell it, but technically, that's what it is, serving some of London's most delicious crispy-based pizzas, all one hundred per cent organic. The margherita won 'the tastiest fast feast in the world' in recent industry awards, but the pizzas are just part of the magic. Owners Ann Shore and Lee Hollingworth have backgrounds in fashion styling (her) and architecture (him), and Story's aesthetic is so ravishing you'll want to go home and copy it. Underneath the lofty beamed ceiling sit two communal tables of bleached and white-painted wood. Vintage mirrors are propped against the bare white walls, with clusters of beeswax candles arranged beside them. It's easy to see Ann's *Vogue*-stylist eye at work. There's more of her creativity on display next door, in a corner shop that serves as her showroom for private commissions. Only Ann could make a chandelier fashioned from oyster shells, crystals and twigs utterly covetable. Come for a pizza, go home inspired.

123 Bethnal Green Road
E2 7DG
Tel 0791 819 7352
www.storydeli.com

15*

16*

16*

16*

15* SHOREDITCH HOUSE

Not a member of Shoreditch House, the private members' club that's part of the global Soho House group? Get a room ... literally. Book yourself an overnight stay in one of the club's gorgeously bijou Shoreditch Rooms, and full access is yours. Even if the club was not attached, this would be a fantastic place to stay. Walls are clad in pale grey wood boarding, dark hessian matting takes the place of carpet, and you hang your clothes on a series of chunky hooks at picture-rail level. The rooms exude beach-hut chic, with a casual luxe feel that you don't often find in a city hotel. Make sure you make full use of the club's facilities (you can sign in a friend as well) with drinks up on the roof garden, then dinner in the buzzy House Kitchen restaurant. And the best bit? An early-morning swim in the 15-metre rooftop pool. Always heated, it's a perfect start to the day, whatever the time of year.

Ebor Street
E1 6AW
Tel 0207 739 5040
www.shoreditchhouse.com

16* ACE HOTEL LONDON SHOREDITCH

One of the world's hippest hotel names has landed in London, and where else could it set up home but hipster central Shoreditch? Arrive in the early evening and you'll find a DJ on the decks as you check in, surrounded by Shoreditch's beautiful people at the always-busy bar. Add the local artists' work exhibited on the walls, a photo booth and the mix of sofas, armchairs and a long communal work table with workers hunched over their MacBooks, and the vibe is more private gathering than hotel lobby. If it sounds slightly intimidating, fear not. The Ace is blessed with some of the most charming staff in London. You'll feel welcomed from the minute you walk through the door. The mood continues in the rooms. Conceived to feel like a friend's Shoreditch apartment, they come complete with a turntable and vinyl records. Back downstairs, the Hoi Polloi restaurant is run by the skilled team behind **Bistrotheque** (see page 175). And the food? Outstanding. It might have taken a while for the Ace brand to reach London, but it was worth the wait.

100 Shoreditch High Street
E1 6JQ
Tel 0207 613 9800
www.acehotel.com

17✳ 40 WINKS

You will never have slept anywhere like 40 Winks. Interior designer David Carter rents two B&B rooms (one single, one double) at the top of his 1700s Queen Anne townhouse, and the experience of entering his creatively extraordinary world is breathtaking. The house is, quite simply, magical. Every surface, every nook and cranny, has been filled with objects and art. There's too much to take in at once; you have to sit and gaze at a room for a while to appreciate all the details. The more you look, the more you notice. Crystals, lace, mirrors, velvets, shells, corals, feathers—they're all used to adorn the house. The main bedroom is styled like the boudoir of a well-travelled lady, complete with a pile of old suitcases with handwritten luggage labels and a sailor's hat. Everything has a story to tell. Book well ahead to avoid disappointment—the house is a favourite with visiting magazine teams shooting in London—and make sure you have a good look around. London's most original check-in, without a doubt.

109 Mile End Road
E1 4UJ
Tel 0207 790 0259
www.40winks.org

167

brix smith-start

Start London is where the cool girls go to shop. Is it any wonder, when you look at the CV of its owner, Brix Smith-Start? Guitarist and singer with legendary 1980s Brit band The Fall. Actress. TV presenter. Boutique owner. The woman has cool coming out of every pore. And it shows in the clothes she stocks. This is properly grown-up luxury shopping—pricey labels, beautiful setting, knowledgeable staff. Brix has a perfect eye when it comes to cherry-picking the best of the new season trends, and then displaying them irresistibly. Your credit card might not be happy, but your wardrobe will be.

START LONDON
42–44 Rivington Street EC2A 3BN ❋ 0207 033 3951 ❋ www.start-london.com

'When you stand
in Hyde Park you
feel like you are
in the country'

How would you define London style?
Free, quirky, creative and gracefully discreet.

Where do you go in London to be inspired?
Most definitely Hyde Park and The
Serpentine Gallery (www.serpentinegalleries.
org) on a Sunday with my husband and my
dogs. When you stand in Hyde Park you feel
like you are in the country.

Your favourite local places?
So many. **Bistrotheque** (see page 175) is
the epicentre of the cool fashion crowd. It's
like Soho, New York in the 1980s. They have
a fantastic tranny cabaret and it's always
a brilliant night out with wonderful food.
White Cube (www.whitecube.com), an
awesome gallery with ground-breaking,
mentally stimulating, food for thought.
Saf (www.safrestaurant.co.uk), a great
vegan restaurant, so tasty you almost can't
believe it's meat-free! I always feel so good
after eating there. Rochelle School Canteen
(www.arnoldandhenderson.com) which is a
well-kept secret. Tucked away behind a gate,

it's a gem to put in your restaurant black book. And finally, The George & Dragon (2–4 Hackney Road, E2 7NS, tel 0207 012 1100), the best gay pub in London. A total Shoreditch hangout.

Best place for a drink?

The rooftop garden at **Shoreditch House** (see page 165), where my beverage of choice is an espresso martini ... but only one!

Where do you go in London to relax?

The Cowshed spa at Shoreditch House for luxury treatments.

Favourite cultural sights?

Tate Modern (www.tate.org.uk), the V&A (www.vam.ac.uk), the Serpentine Gallery in the summer time, **Columbia Road** (see page 98), Covent Garden flower market (www. newcoventgardenmarket.com) in the mornings, and The Globe Theatre (www.shakespearesglobe.com).

Describe your perfect out-and-about weekend?

I get out of the city! I go to the beach, to Camber Sands in East Sussex, with my dogs and my husband. Nestled among the sand dunes, we watch the clouds pass.

And what about a weekend in London?

I always work on Saturday, so the only day off I really have is Sunday and, creatures of habit, we spend it the same way every single week. We wake up early with the dogs and have breakfast at Jamie Oliver's Fifteen (www.fifteen.net). We then drive with the dogs to Hyde Park or Kensington Gardens and do a long family walk all the way around the park. We then drive to Marylebone High Street and visit the Farmer's Market to get fruit, veg and goodies for the week to come. We also usually visit **Daunt Books** (see page 215) and each buy a book for the week. We get back in the car and drive to Whole Foods in Camden (www. wholefoodsmarket.com), do the rest of our weekly shopping and head home to spend the rest of the afternoon reading, watching TV and cuddling our dogs.

Your favourite breakfast spot?

The Rivington Grill (www. rivingtongrill.co.uk) is like our local café. Even though it's owned by Caprice Holdings and has a glamorous clientele (the crème de la crème of Brit art stars, for example), there's something relaxed and unpretentious about it, and the food is utterly delicious in a classically British way.

Top three things that every visitor to London should do?

Apparently Madame Tussauds—the line never ends! Seriously though, Tate Modern (www.tate.org.uk), and take in a play in the West End. And I love the Tower of London (www.hrp.org.uk/toweroflondon) for its history and fantasy.

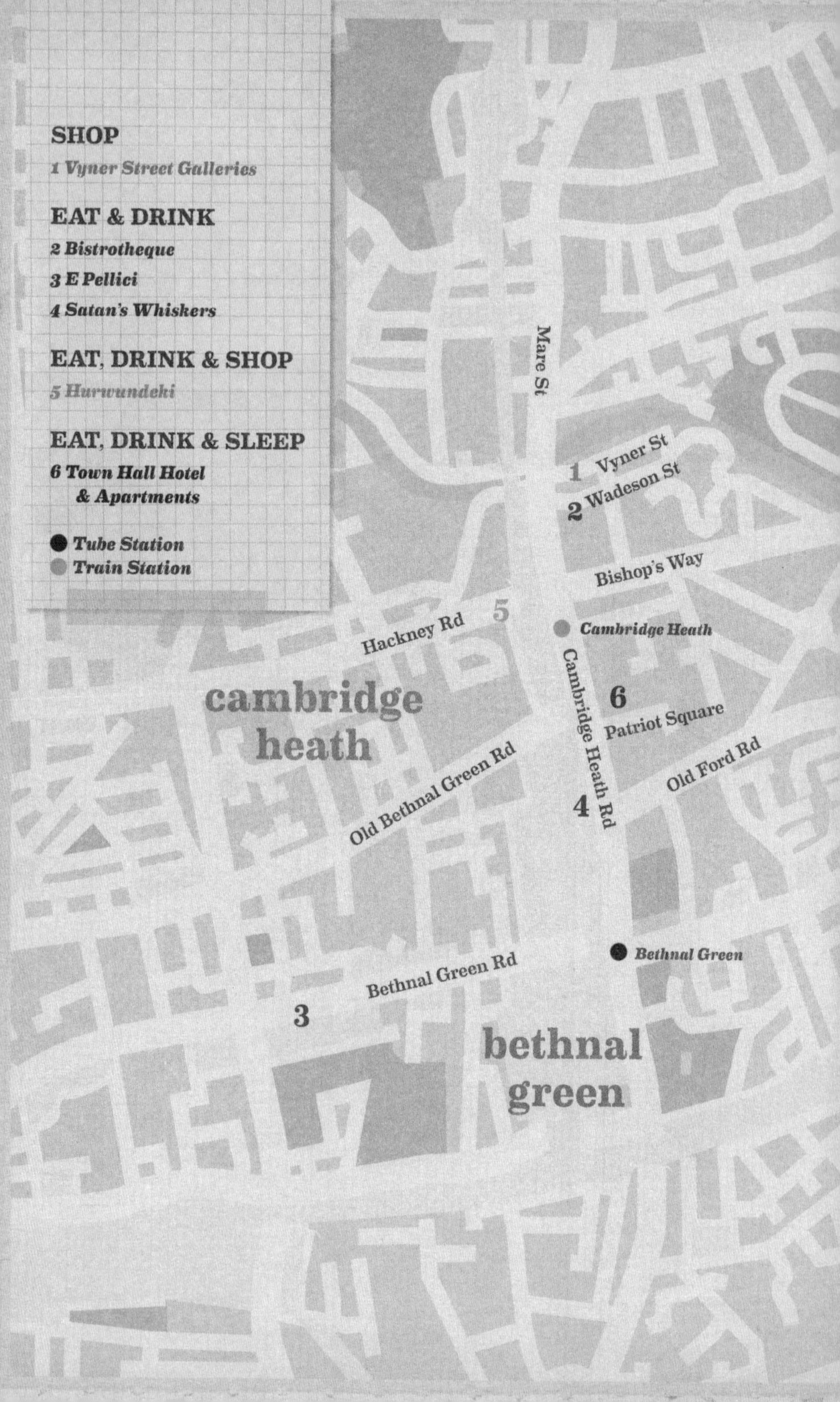

SHOP
1 Vyner Street Galleries
EAT & DRINK
2 Bistrotheque
3 E Pellici
4 Satan's Whiskers
EAT, DRINK & SHOP
5 Hurwundeki
EAT, DRINK & SLEEP
6 Town Hall Hotel
& Apartments
Tube Station
Train Station
Mare St
Vyner St
Wadeson St
Bishop's Way
Hackney Rd
Cambridge Heath
Cambridge Heath Rd
Patriot Square
cambridge
heath
Old Bethnal Green Rd
Old Ford Rd
Bethnal Green
Bethnal Green Rd
bethnal
green
1
2
3
4
5
6

bethnal green

In the heart of London's East End, Bethnal Green is a melting pot. With a history of French Huguenot, Jewish and Bangladeshi influences, it represents everything that is so special about the city's multicultural DNA. Add to that the more recent influence of the contemporary art scene and the hub of young artists living and working in the area, and you have an intriguing mix. Rough and ready around the edges, it's worth a visit just to have a drink in the splendour of the restored Town Hall Hotel. Neighbouring Shoreditch is a short stroll, and the centre of London a quick Tube ride, making this a very well-connected spot.

1* VYNER STREET GALLERIES

The last thing you expect to find down this nondescript cobbled street is a cluster of cool, contemporary art galleries. Don't be deceived by appearances. It may look like a road of warehouses, but ring on the doorbells and you'll find yourself in some of London's edgiest art spaces. **Wilkinson** (50–58 Vyner Street, London E2 9DQ, tel 0208 980 2662, www.wilkinsongallery. com) is the sleekest of the lot, all polished concrete floors and cavernous white exhibition spaces. **HADA Contemporary** (21 Vyner Street, London E2 9DG, tel 0208 983 7700, www.hadacontemporary. com) showcases artists from East Asia, with an emphasis on Korea, while **Vyner Street Gallery** (23 Vyner Street, E2 9DG, tel 0797 048 4316, www. vynerstreetgallery.co.uk) has a packed schedule of emerging and student artists' shows. For the full experience, time your visit for the first Thursday of the month, when the East London gallery scene unites for last-night events, talks, workshops and private views (www.firstthursdays.co.uk).

2* BISTROTHEQUE

In 2004, this was one of the pioneer openings in what was then a grotty, industrial wasteland. Certainly not a first-on-your-list area for a cool night out. But the owners were ahead of their time and ten years on, Bistrotheque is an institution. The street still isn't pretty, and the neighbouring buildings still look like shabby warehouses, but no-one wonders anymore if there really is a restaurant in surrounds like these. Perennially packed, Bistrotheque is loved by locals and visitors alike. The restaurant is an airy white space, little changed since the building's industrial days, save for white tiling on the walls and designer lighting hanging from the exposed steel girders. Always busy for weekend brunch (with a pianist accompaniment), there's also a private dining room downstairs, with room to seat 96. No surprise it's one of East London's favourite hipster wedding venues.

23–27 Wadeson Street
E2 9DR
Tel 0208 983 7900
www.bistrotheque.com

3✱ E PELLICI

For a sense of what turn-of-the-century Bethnal Green was like, stop off at this tiny, crowded café. There's a reason this squeezy, wood-panelled, low-ceilinged space has been granted a Grade II listing. Opened in 1900, it has remained pretty much unchanged, a gem of Art Deco style run by the same family from the start. Marquetry panelling on the inside and Vitrolite glass frontage on the outside, it's a little piece of history among the internet cafés and kebab shops on this strip of road. And the Italian food's not bad either.
332 Bethnal Green Road
E2 OAG
Tel 0207 739 4873

4✱ SATAN'S WHISKERS

With a Ouija board on the wall, a 'unicorn' skeleton and several striking taxidermy pieces, this is no ordinary bar. Add in a blaring hip-hop sound track, seriously good cocktails (the Satan's Aperitif of Aperol, clementine and prosecco is a winner) and excellent bar snacks, and you can see why it's packed with happy locals. Decor is quirky industrial, with vintage posters on exposed brick walls and decorative filament light bulbs hanging from the ceiling. There's even free WiFi and posh Jo Malone soap in the loos—the place has class.
343 Cambridge Heath Road
E2 9RA
Tel 0207 739 8362

6✱ TOWN HALL HOTEL & APARTMENTS

This disused Edwardian town hall was brought back to life in 2011 and is now one of London's most striking hotels. The Grade II listed building has been beautifully restored and updated to create a sleek, modern place to stay that combines all the grand elements of its heritage with decidedly 21st-century touches. From the neoclassical frontage to the inlaid marbling and sweeping staircase in the reception, there's a sense of history wherever you look. But this is no stuffy stuck-in-a-time-warp establishment; far from it. The work of local East End artists is championed throughout the building, thanks to an open commission scheme that invited them to create site-specific work. Keep an eye out for Debbie Lawson's *Persian Moose* sculpture, fashioned from antique carpets. Not what the Edwardians would have been used to. Generously proportioned bedrooms feature lovely original parquet floors, high ceilings and lots of daylight. To be totally wowed, sneak a peak at the De Montfort Suite, a huge warehouse-sized space in the former council chamber, complete with a dining table for twenty and a glass-panelled staircase leading up to the sleeping area. The hotel's restaurants include the casual Corner Room, which is perfect for a relaxed lunch. If you're in the area, make sure you pop in.

Patriot Square
E2 9NF
Tel 0207 871 0460
www.townhallhotel.com

'Generously proportioned bedrooms feature lovely original parquet floors, high ceilings and lots of daylight'

179

ki-chul lee

Can there be anywhere else in London where you can get a haircut and a Korean meal? Doubtful. But then Ki-chul Lee is a pretty one-off character. The Korean-born hairdresser-turned-designer-turned-café owner is a man of many talents, and Hurwundeki shows off his eclectic skill set. The man himself can be found in the hair salon out the back, where the barber's chairs are lined up on a rough stone floor, the walls are crumbling brick, and chandeliers add some unexpected glamour. So far, so quirky. Then there's the café, serving delicious Korean dishes in the midst of junkshop decor— think old paintings, stag heads and box-framed taxidermy on the walls. Unusual, but it works.

HURWUNDEKI
299 Railway Arches, Cambridge Heath Road E2 9HA ✳ 0207 749 0638

> '*London is so multicultural that you can eat any kind of food here*'

Where do you go in London to be inspired?

I particularly like Portobello Road market on a Friday—the day when all the antique traders go. It helps me to understand the past and also to think about the future. I also like to find open spaces within this busy city, and I often go to Richmond Park (www.royalparks.org.uk/parks/richmond-park) if I need some mental and physical space.

Your favourite local places?

I've always loved Brick Lane, Columbia Road (see page 98) and Broadway Market (see page 118). Around Brick Lane there are lots of small art and design studios, which I find inspiring. Columbia Road has the flower market, but also so many nice little shops selling different things. Broadway Market is the most special, I think. I like the nearby Regent's Canal, the shops and the great coffee.

Describe your perfect out-and-about weekend?

I have two kids, a girl and boy, and as I work too many hours, I hold all my free time for them. We often go to galleries as a family, such as the Serpentine (www.serpentinegalleries.org) and Tate Modern (www.tate.org.uk). Somerset House (www.somersethouse.org.uk) has some good exhibitions too.

What's in your secret shopping address book?

I like the car boot sales (www.capitalcarboot.com) in Pimlico and Battersea on a Sunday. I also look around the local vintage stores on Brick Lane. My favourites are Rokit (www.rokit.co.uk) and Beyond Retro (www.beyondretro.com), which is huge. Also, Traid (www.traid.org.uk) in Notting Hill.

Best place for a weekend supper?

On Sundays I often go to the good Vietnamese restaurants on Kingsland Road. Tay Do Café (www.taydo.co.uk) is particularly good. Also Upper Street in Islington is an amazing place to walk of a weekend; I really like Le Mercury (www.lemercury.co.uk) there. I always look for great value for money, which is what we offer at Hurwundeki.

Best place for a drink?

I go to nice cafés that aren't too busy. I like Stories (www.storiesonbroadway.com) on Broadway Market, and also the Hackney Bureau (www.hackneybureau.com) near Hurwundeki—it's a really lovely place to relax with a nice coffee

Top three things that every visitor to London should do?

Get a day's travel card and take any bus, without having a clue where you're going. London is huge and it's good to get lost and discover your own part of it, away from the hustle and bustle. Visitors may think the English have no idea about food, but London is so multicultural that you can eat any kind of food here. I believe it's the capital of world, not just the capital of England. Each area caters to a different cuisine so it depends what you like, but Upper Street in Islington, Wardour Street in Soho and Brick Lane near Bethnal Green are good places to start. Finally, come and see us at Hurwundeki!

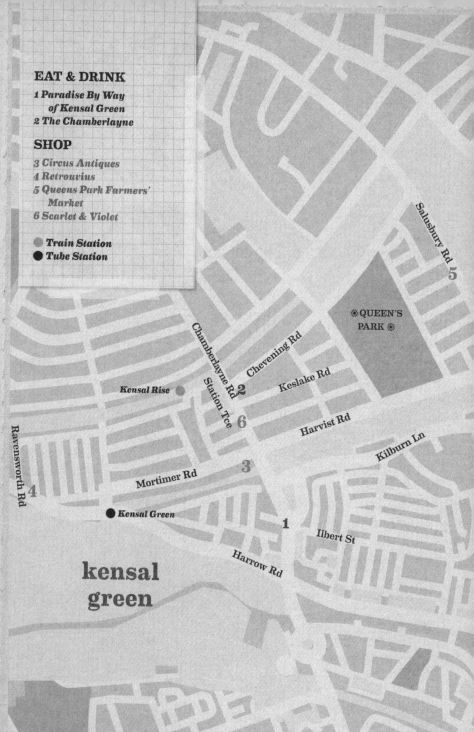

EAT & DRINK

1 *Paradise By Way of Kensal Green*
2 *The Chamberlayne*

SHOP

3 *Circus Antiques*
4 *Retrouvius*
5 *Queens Park Farmers' Market*
6 *Scarlet & Violet*

● *Train Station*
● *Tube Station*

Salusbury Rd

❋QUEEN'S PARK❋

5

Chamberlayne Rd

Chevening Rd

Kensal Rise

Station Tce

2

Keslake Rd

6

Harvist Rd

Kilburn Ln

3

Ravensworth Rd

Mortimer Rd

4

Kensal Green

1

Ilbert St

Harrow Rd

kensal green

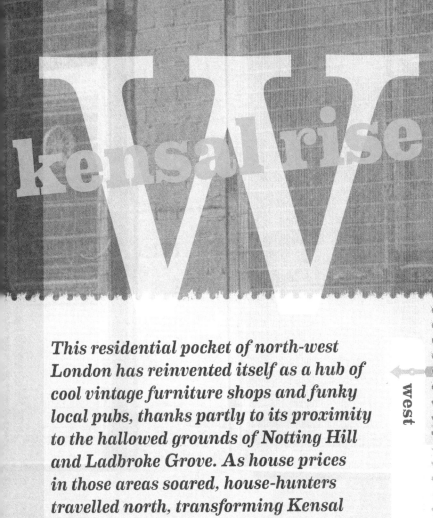

kensal rise

This residential pocket of north-west London has reinvented itself as a hub of cool vintage furniture shops and funky local pubs, thanks partly to its proximity to the hallowed grounds of Notting Hill and Ladbroke Grove. As house prices in those areas soared, house-hunters travelled north, transforming Kensal Rise into an unexpectedly desirable spot. A sprinkling of celebrity locals like Jade Jagger and Daniel Craig (the actor was a Kensal Riser for a while) has also helped; the chance of a bit of star-spotting in the local pub makes it well worth a visit.

1✳ PARADISE BY WAY OF KENSAL GREEN

Far more than just a humble local pub, this ornately decorated Victorian drinking establishment has hosted local supermodel Sophie Dahl's birthday celebrations and seen Jade Jagger take to the decks as DJ. With two bars and a restaurant downstairs, and three more bars and private dining spaces upstairs, it acts as a bar, restaurant, comedy venue and nightclub all in one. It's even launched life-drawing classes featuring burlesque dancers as models. The decor is ornately shabby chic, with chandeliers, candelabras, squashy sofas and decorative wallpaper. Book in advance for the main restaurant— the menu's impressive—or just spend a night in the bar sipping espresso martinis. Also worth checking out is the once-a-month Rag & Bow vintage sale, held on a Saturday.

19 Kilburn Lane
W10 4AE
Tel 0208 969 0098
www.theparadise.co.uk

2✶ THE CHAMBERLAYNE

Pubs like this are what London excels at: easygoing atmosphere, just-stylish-enough decor and simple, delicious food. You'll find locals of all ages here, from the old-timers nursing pints at the bar, to a younger crowd in search of drinks and dinner. Add a few children into the mix and you've got the perfect neighbourhood hangout. Up until a few years ago, this was just another dingy pub, but a sleek makeover gave it stripped-wood floors and cool industrial-style furnishings, and it's been packed ever since. Food-wise, it's all about the meat, with huge pride taken in offering the finest British beef, sourced daily from Smithfield meat market. The steaks are some of the best you'll taste on a pub menu. The organic roast chicken is pretty good, too.
83 Chamberlayne Rd
NW10 3ND
Tel 0208 960 4311
www.thechamberlayne.com

3✶ CIRCUS ANTIQUES

Circus Antiques has a chic selection of beautifully restored vintage furniture. Don't expect to uncover any quirky bargains here, but if you're in the market for 1950s French chandeliers, Art Deco mirrored dressing tables, or even a 1940s oak haberdashery shop counter, this is the place to come.
60 Chamberlayne Road
NW10 3JH
Tel 0208 968 8244
www.circusantiques.co.uk

3*

189

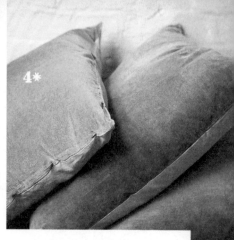

4✳ RETROUVIUS

This architectural salvage and design business is one of the best known in London, with a warehouse crammed full of treasures rescued from building demolitions, house clearances and sales. Metal factory light fittings, timber chairs from a synagogue, a pair of rabbit skeletons—the mix is unlike anything anywhere else. Looking for a row of four fold-up cinema seats? You'll find them here.

1016 Harrow Road
NW10 5NS
Tel 0208 960 6060
www.retrouvius.com

5✳ QUEENS PARK FARMERS' MARKET

This Sunday-morning food market has a reputation as one of the starriest in London. It's not strictly in Kensal Rise, but it's a short walk across Queens Park, and you might catch film star Thandie Newton and her family queuing for the fish man. With stalls selling deliciously fresh produce plus breads, cheeses and cakes, it's no wonder it's packed every week. The barbecue 'sausage in a bun' stall is particularly popular.

Sundays 10 am–2 pm
Salusbury Primary School
Salusbury Road
NW6 6RG
www.lfm.org.uk/markets/queens-park

victoria brotherson

To call Scarlet & Violet a small local florist is to wildly underestimate it. This crammed-to-bursting space is one of the most influential and stylish flower shops in London. Owned by Kensal Rise resident, Victoria Brotherson, its just-picked-from-the-garden seasonal bouquets are regularly ordered by the likes of Nigella Lawson and every magazine editor in town, and it's the first choice for fashionable clients such as Hermès and Louis Vuitton, who use Victoria to decorate their events. For locals, it's a lovely spot to linger while choosing a couple of bunches of blooms. The Christmas wreaths are legendary.

SCARLET & VIOLET
76 Chamberlayne Road NW10 3JJ ✻ **0208 969 9446** ✻ *www.scarletandviolet.com*

'I love looking at front-door colours, window boxes and peeping through the occasional open shutter'

How would you define London style?

I think London is driven creatively by pockets of people all spurring each other on to push the boundaries of their profession. It's not so much about toeing the style lines of elegance and taste, it's more risky and often much more homemade and independent than that.

Where do you go in London to be inspired?

As part of my job I go to private homes— these are a real display of London's aesthetic. Even just from the outside, I love looking at front-door colours, window boxes and peeping through the occasional open shutter.

Your favourite local places?

Portobello and **Golborne Roads** (see page 196) on Fridays and Sundays. They're a hoarder's paradise. Have a little cash in your pocket or you'll miss the most perfect item you've ever seen and it could be a macramé basket, a stash of buttons or an amazing pair of giant urns.

193

Describe your perfect out-and-about weekend?

A dog walk on Hampstead Heath or Hyde Park, and then a sausage roll at **Queens Park Farmers' Market** (see page 190).

What's in your secret shopping address book?

Retrouvius (see page 190), **Circus Antiques** (see page 188), **Howie & Belle** (www.howieandbelle.com) and **Alfies Antique Market** (see page 210). All are a stone's throw from me so if I need a quick shot of inspiration—or a chair for a client to sit on in the office— they are my first port of call. Each is different. Retrouvius has ever-changing, completely amazing but generally large pieces, Howie & Belle has beautifully perfect and weirdly accessible smalls, from chairs to butterflies to lamps, and Alfies is always brilliant inspiration.

Best place for a drink?

The Chamberlayne (see page 188), about 400 yards from my front door, for a delicious steak or half chicken and chips with a Bloody Mary.

Your favourite breakfast spot?

New Toms on Westbourne Grove (www. newtoms.co.uk) is an old favourite for sausage sandwiches, eggs Benedict and a cappuccino.

Where do you go in London to relax?

Richmond Park (www.royalparks.org. uk/parks/richmond-park) is the perfect place to go to switch off. Once inside the boundary roads, you are kind of transported to Narnia. Even with the families of cyclists it is an amazing place that always has quiet and peaceful pockets.

Favourite cultural sights?

The Summer Exhibition at the Royal Academy (www.royalacademy.org.uk) makes me feel alive and refreshed. The Turbine Hall at Tate Modern (www.tate.org.uk) for the space and the calm, and The Wallace Collection (www.wallacecollection.org)—if I go alone I transport myself back to a time without any responsibility and just gaze and enjoy a wander.

Top three things that every visitor to London should do?

Have afternoon tea at Claridge's (www. claridges.co.uk), get on an open-top bus and see all the amazing architecture we have, and walk up **Columbia Road** early on a Sunday morning (see page 98).

195

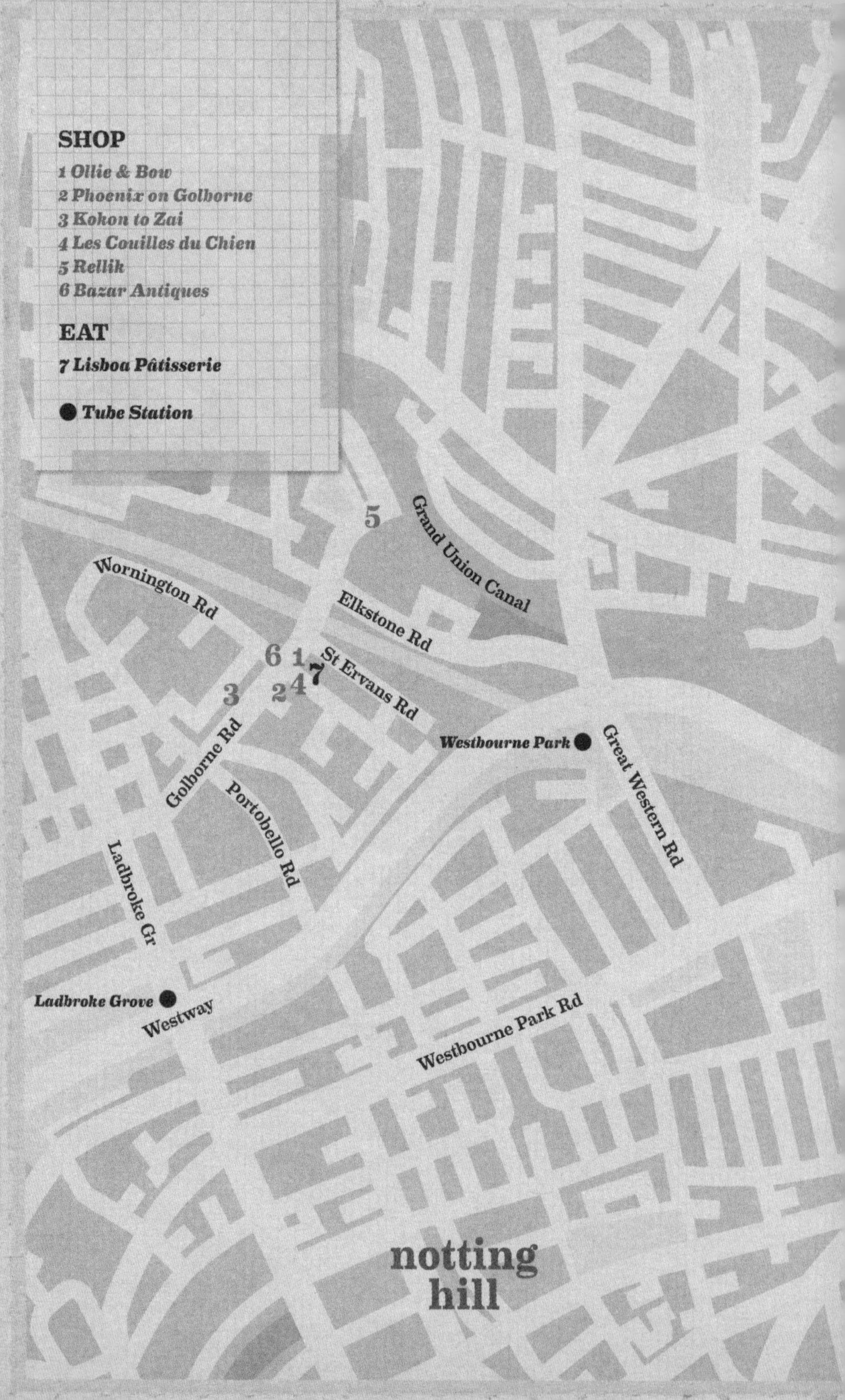
SHOP
1 Ollie & Bow
2 Phoenix on Golborne
3 Kokon to Zai
4 Les Couilles du Chien
5 Rellik
6 Bazar Antiques
EAT
7 Lisboa Pâtisserie
Tube Station
Grand Union Canal
Wornington Rd
Elkstone Rd
St Ervans Rd
Golborne Rd
Portobello Rd
Westbourne Park
Great Western Rd
Ladbroke Gr
Ladbroke Grove
Westway
Westbourne Park Rd
notting hill
5
6
1
7
3
2
4

notting hill

Londoners tend to avoid Portobello Market—too full of tourists buying overpriced antiques and trying to find the bookshop run by Hugh Grant in Notting Hill. Little do the visiting crowds realise that they're missing the area's real treasure, Golborne Road. At the north end of Portobello Road, further than most tourists ever venture, this short street is where you'll find those in the know on a Friday and Saturday, browsing the kerbside bric-a-brac stalls and hunting for interiors treasures at the various antique furniture shops. It is very much Notting Hill for locals, so do yourself a favour and join them. One tip: a lot of the shops are open at weekends only, so check with them before you visit.

1✳ OLLIE & BOW

If this place were any more crammed, you wouldn't be able to get through the door. A mix of Art Deco, retro and random shabby-chic items, it's an irresistible spot to rummage and hunt down something unique for your home. Some pieces are obviously stylish—a 1930s oak-and-glass-fronted haberdasher's cupboard—while others are quirkily eccentric; dentist's chair, anyone? Make sure you venture down to the basement back room. Dimly lit and piled high with what looks like junk, it might just be where you uncover some treasure.

69 Golborne Road
W10 5NP
Tel 0776 879 0725

3✳ KOKON TO ZAI

This beautiful old butcher's shop is a Victorian treasure. With its tiled frontage and mosaic entrance, it's a unique shopping experience from the second you cross the threshold. Inside, the eclectic mood continues. Thistle-design tiles, a solid marble counter top and a delicately mosaic-tiled floor all make it worth a visit for the interior alone. The merchandise will intrigue you. A mix of fashion and lifestyle items, the overall mood is *Alice In Wonderland* meets *Pirates of the Caribbean*, with skull motives, stag beatles, feathers, candles and butterflies. No wonder the likes of Kate Moss and Jade Jagger are fans. Both have bought artwork of a stage set fashioned from cut-up pieces of the *London Illustrated Post*. Stunning.

86 Golborne Road
W10 5PS
Tel 0208 960 3736
www.kokontozai.co.uk

4✳LES COUILLES DU CHIEN

Another piled-high treasure trove, but
with slightly more space to view items than
some of its Golborne Road neighbours. It's
no wonder that sixty per cent of the business
is done with other dealers; owner Jerome
Dodd has been here for over 20 years and
he has an impeccable eye for a good buy
(and a good sense of humour when it comes
to shop names). From beautifully chosen
pieces of furniture to exquisite chandeliers
and mirrors, and smaller items like pieces
of coral and butterflies displayed under
Victorian domes, the shop is a delight.
Even the stuffed badger that greets you
on arrival manages to look stylish.
65 Golborne Road
W10 5NP
Tel 0208 968 0099
www.lescouillesduchien.com

5✳RELLIK

The mothership of seriously collectible
vintage, Rellik is where aficionados come
for pieces by some of the greatest names
in fashion history. Ossie Clark, Yves Saint
Laurent, Chanel, Pucci, Christian Dior ...
You'll find them all on the crammed rails
of this tiny shop, plus an enticing selection
of accessories, from affordable costume
jewellery to pricier designs. Don't be put
off by the location—on a scruffy corner
surrounded by less than salubrious high-rise
housing; this is *the* spot for a vintage buy that
you'll treasure.
8 Golborne Road
W10 5NW
Tel 0208 962 0089
www.relliklondon.co.uk

201

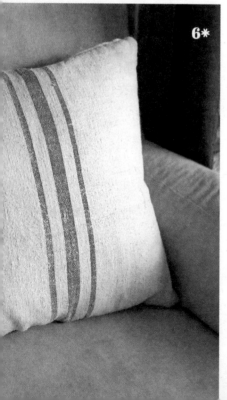

6✳BAZAR ANTIQUES

A contrast to the theatricality of
many of the other shops on the strip,
this is a pocket of chic French charm.
Specialising in homewares from
France from around 1850 to 1950, it has
everything from beautiful iron garden
furniture and a set of old science lab
chairs to larger armoires and dressers.
There are also plenty of cheaper pieces
of glass and crockery. A lovely, tranquil
shopping experience.
82 Golborne Road
W10 5PS
Tel 0208 969 6262

7✳LISBOA PÂTISSERIE

Not glam, not stylish, but the purveyors
of the most delicious Portuguese custard
tarts in London. Do not leave Golborne
Road without stopping off for one.
57 Golborne Road
W10 5NR
Tel 0208 968 5242

6*

jess gildersleve

At Phoenix on Golborne, Jess Gildersleve has assembled a gorgeously edited selection of vintage and antique homewares, dating from 1800 to the mid-century. Her aim is to mix useful bits of furniture, such as dining tables and dressers, with cheaper, quirkier items like painted watering cans, vases and bread bins. All of it displayed to perfection, thanks to Jess's bang-on eye for styling. She personally sources all the pieces, and then restores them, often to customers' individual specs. And if her skills inspire you, she also runs furniture painting and restoration workshops for anyone wishing to do it themselves.

PHOENIX ON GOLBORNE
67 Golborne Road W10 5NP ✻ 0208 964 8123 ✻ www.phoenixongolborne.co.uk

'Just travelling a few miles, it feels like you're in a new city'

How would you define London style?
Adventurous and confident, but never pretentious.

Where do you go to be inspired?
Pretty much anywhere in London, it's in a constant state of flux—whenever you go back to an area there's something different to see, eat or do. Just by travelling a few miles, it feels like you're in a new city; different people, architecture, food and shops. Soho's always great for people watching, as is around Brick Lane. Oh, and Liberty of course (www.liberty.co.uk).

Your favourite local places?
Kokon to Zai (see page 198) is always a feast for the eyes, Golborne Deli (www. golbornedeli.com) for breakfast and coffee, **Lisboa Pâtisserie** (see page 202) for their famous custard tarts, Trini Flava for cheap, hearty Trinidadian food (on the corner of Golborne and Portobello Roads on Friday and Saturday), and Jane Bourvis (www.janebourvis.co.uk) for stunning vintage couture.

205

Describe your perfect out-and-about weekend?

Start by having a wander down Portobello Road, coffee from Coffee Plant (www.coffee.uk.com), then some pampering at Portobello Girl Beauty (www.portobellogirl-beauty.co.uk), dinner and drinks at Santo (www.santovillage.com), all on Portobello Road. Then on Sunday, a walk on Hampstead Heath followed by food and quiz at the **Bull & Last** (see page 13).

What's in your secret shopping address book?

Portobello market for vintage clothes on a Friday morning—so much better than Saturdays; **Scarlet & Violet** (see page 192) in Kensal Rise for flowers, and Merchant Archive (www.merchantarchive.com) on Kensington Park Road.

Where's the best place for a weekend supper?

Either Barrica (www.barrica. co.uk) for superb tapas and delicious wine, Launceston Place (www. launcestonplace-restaurant.co.uk) for a special occasion, or for top-notch steak head to **The Chamberlayne** (see page 188) in Kensal Rise.

Best place for a drink?

For a post-work glass of wine and people watching, you can't beat an outside table at Pizza East Portobello (www.pizzaeast.com). The bar at National Theatre (www.nationaltheatre. org.uk) is lovely for a glass of something fizzy with a super view, or Crate Brewery in Hackney Wick (www. cratebrewery.com) for home-brewed beer, right on the canal—even better if the sun's out.

Top three things that every visitor to London should do?

Go east (Shoreditch) and west (Notting Hill/Golborne Road)—amazing but so different, and you need both to experience London properly. Take a walk through Regent's Park up to Primrose Hill; the view never fails to impress. And hop on a boat from Embankment Pier to Greenwich— it's great to see the sights from a different perspective.

'It's great to see the sights from a different perspective'

SHOP

1 Margaret Howell
2 Alfies Antique Market
3 Andrew Nebbett Antiques
4 Matches
5 Daunt Books
6 VV Rouleaux
7 Le Labo
8 KJs Laundry

EAT & DRINK

9 Purl
10 The Providores

EAT & SHOP

11 Comptoir Libanais
12 La Fromagerie

● Tube Station
● Train Station

REGENT'S PARK

QUEEN MARY'S GARDENS

lisson grove

Park Rd

3 2

Church St

Lisson Gr

Regent's Park ●

● Baker Street

Marylebone

Marylebone Rd

● Edgware Road

Marylebone High St

7 Devonshire st

Paddington St

Weymouth St

Seymour Pl

Gloucester Pl

Baker St

12 5
4

10

New Cavendish S

Blandford St 9

6

George St

marylebone

8

11

Wigmore St

Thayer St

marylebone

The Great British High Street is an endangered species. In an era of chain stores and identikit rows of shops—same coffee chain, same fast-fashion shop, same supermarket—Marylebone High Street and its surrounds is a rare thing. Packed with small, independent shops and an atmosphere all its own, it is one of London's most popular shopping parades and together with the surrounding streets, a lovely part of town for a wander.

1 ✳ MARGARET HOWELL

This shop is the ultimate in understated British good taste. Everything about it is quietly just right. Margaret Howell is known for her beautifully crafted, elegant clothes, and the shop reflects that. Lots of natural light, white walls and old, worn floorboards—simple. There's no interior design 'concept' here. Instead, you'll find the perfect tailored shirt, the best-cut pair of trousers and a chunky cashmere knit. Oh, and maybe something vintage for the home; the designer is passionate about 20th-century design and showcases some beautiful furniture here, alongside a few carefully chosen modern bits and pieces of homeware. Not cheap but very classy.
34 Wigmore Street
W1U 2RS
Tel 0207 009 9009
www.margarethowell.co.uk

2 ✳ ALFIES ANTIQUE MARKET

Ask any fashionable London shopper where is top of their little black book of must-visits, and the chances are Alfies will be on the list. More than just a shop, it's a rabbit warren of some of the city's very best dealers in antiques, vintage and 20th-century design. It's also London's largest indoor market, covering four floors and over 35,000 square feet. The range of choice is bewildering, with literally everything covered, from a fun piece of leopard-print 1950s clothing to an astonishing antique Murano glass chandelier. Big, small, affordable, out-of-this-world, it's all here. The place is a day trip in itself. The location—a decidedly scruffy market street—may look unpromising but don't be put off. This is one of London's most exciting shopping locations. Step inside and be blown away.
13–25 Church Street
NW8 8DT
Tel 0207 723 6066
www.alfiesantiques.com

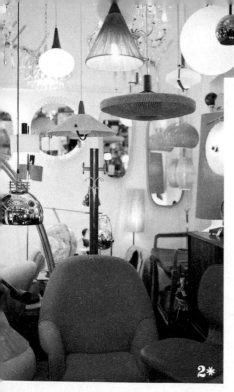

4*

3*

3*

3* ANDREW NEBBETT ANTIQUES

Alfies has many antique shops as neighbours, all of them worth a look. This one stands out for its clever edit of classic and quirky pieces, all in a sleek warehouse-like setting. It's quite a contrast to the higgledy-piggledy chaos of Alfies next door. Sleek leather Chesterfield sofas and elegant antique mirrors sit alongside more random finds, such as old glass pharmacy bottles and a late 19th-century mahogany hotel reception newspaper rack. And don't miss the window displays; there's always a piece of inventive styling that will maybe give you an idea or two to try at home.

35–37 Church Street
NW8 8ES
Tel 0207 723 2303
www.andrewnebbett.com

4* MATCHES

Two words: high fashion. The sleekest, most fabulous, most budget-busting names are all here. Everything a fashion mecca should be, it's small enough to feel intimate and big enough to offer the very best of every catwalk trend. And the beauty is in the details; a coffee machine and delicate china cups sit on a marble counter top, and there are sofas to sink into if your credit card is feeling weary. Even the iPad-toting assistants are perfectly designed. You might wince at the prices, but come and admire it as a temple of high-end shopping.

87 Marylebone High Street
W1U 4QU
Tel 0207 487 5400
www.matchesfashion.com

4*

213

5❋

5❋ DAUNT BOOKS

In this age of Amazon deals, a local
bookshop is a rare sight, and Londoners
treasure Daunt Books. With its dark-
green-and-wood Edwardian frontage,
this looks exactly how you imagine a
traditional bookshop should look, and
it doesn't disappoint inside. The star
attraction is the long, oak gallery at the
back, with a skylight running the length
of the room—more university library than
high-street bookshop. Leather armchairs
encourage lingering, and the worn
parquet floors add to the cosy, collegiate
feel. As for the books, this was originally
a travel branch, and one of the first
bookshops to group books by countries—
with not just guides but literature, design
and general interest titles about that part
of the world clustered together. Daunt also
stocks general fiction and does a sterling
job promoting local authors. Much more
fun than browsing Amazon online.
83 Marylebone High Street
W1U 4QW
Tel 0207 224 2295
www.dauntbooks.co.uk

6❋ VV ROULEAUX

Be prepared for a wonderland of ribbons,
trimmings, laces, feathers, flowers and
even Christmas decorations in this
crammed corner shop. No surprise that
fashion and interiors stylists can't stay
away—it's irresistible. You'll find reel
upon reel of coloured ribbons in every
texture and every width imaginable,
cards wound with strings of crystal
beading, pieces of lace and even huge
curtain tassels in a choice of rainbow
colours. You might not have a single
use for a length of velvet ribbon in an
exquisite shade of soft pink or blue,
but you'll want some. Small beaded
peacocks? Of course you want a pair
of those to put on your Christmas tree.
And for any Kate Middleton wannabes,
the shop offers a headdress-making
service, using its considerable stock of
fake flowers and feathers. Just the thing
for the next royal wedding.
102 Marylebone Lane
W1U 2QD
Tel 0207 224 5179
www.vvrouleaux.com

ROSE 31
100ml 3,4 FL.OZ.
eau de parfum / vaporisateur
natural spray
Compounded: in London by Camelia
SASKA GRAVILLE
Fresh until: 02/10/2012
LE LABO London · 28A Devonshire Street, London
Hand made in USA · 233 Elizabeth Street, New York

7✳ LE LABO

This apothecary-like shop is the home of cult perfume brand Le Labo. If you're used to picking up a bottle of your favourite scent in Duty Free, be prepared for a whole new experience. Once you've chosen your blend, it gets hand-finished in front of you, with a lab-coated employee blending and mixing the final oils and then printing a personalised label. It's quite an operation. Shelves of medicinal bottles, jars of dried ingredients, and a corner glass 'lab' of Pyrex glass jars and pipettes tell you that this is somewhere that takes fragrance very seriously. Sit up at the white-tiled, metal-topped counter and watch it all unfold. Oh, and the smells are something very special too—there's a reason why a bottle from Le Labo is a favourite with beauty insiders.

28a Devonshire Street
W1G 6PS
Tel 0203 441 1535
www.lelabofragrances.com

9✳ PURL

Head down some unpromising-looking stairs to the basement of this Georgian house and you'll enter one of London's most enticing bars. Channelling the spirit of a New York speakeasy, the low-ceilinged, dimly lit space is a sexy, cosy rabbit warren ... with killer cocktails. Booking is essential, especially if you want one of the booths tucked into the alcoves, each lit by its own chandelier and flickering candles. The house specialty is heritage cocktails served with a modern twist, so expect flourishes such as liquid nitrogen steaming over the glass's rim. More mad professor's lab than swish bar. Or you might be tempted by the silver bowl on the bar top, filled to the brim with the punch of the day—complete with ladle to serve it with. With a barman this good and a venue this intoxicating, prepare to lose track of your night.

50–54 Blandford Street
W1U 7HX
Tel 0207 935 0835
www.purl-london.com

10✳ THE PROVIDORES

A contender for the best cup of coffee in London, Providores is jam-packed with locals every weekend—you'll be lucky to avoid a pavement queue. And no wonder. Brunch in the downstairs Tapa Room is something pretty special, thanks to Kiwi chef–owner Peter Gordon's unique way of combining flavours. Where else would you get poached eggs with whipped yoghurt and hot chilli butter, or Thai basil and lime waffles with tomato, sweetcorn, rocket and avocado chutney and tomato jalapeño chutney? It's not your average British brekkie. In terms of style, a giant bark tapa cloth from Rarotonga sets the tone, with cool light fittings from New Zealand artist Jeremy Cole adding to the eclectic mood. Well worth a bit of a wait for a table, but if you don't want to hang around, you can book brunch in the upstairs Providores space; it's more formal and less funky, but the food's still delicious.
109 Marylebone High Street
W1U 4RX
Tel 0207 935 6175
www.theprovidores.co.uk

11✳ COMPTOIR LIBANAIS

This bright, sunny café is part of a chain, but it doesn't feel like it. With a quirky style and interior, it celebrates the fresh and exotic tastes of Middle Eastern cuisine. Yes, the food is delicious, but a big part of its appeal is the colourfully cheerful design. It immediately puts you in a good mood. Bright red metal chairs and tables decorated in geometric blue and turquoise shapes, metal shelves packed with enticing Middle Eastern foods, gorgeous embroidered baskets from Morocco ... It's a touch of the souk in London's West End. Pop in for a lunchtime mezze plate, or for some mint tea and Lebanese sweets in the afternoon. You'll come out smiling.
65 Wigmore Street
W1U 1JT
Tel 0207 935 1110
www.lecomptoir.co.uk

12✷ LA FROMAGERIE

What began as a small cheese shop is now a food empire. Cheese is still at the heart of the business, with an on-site maturing cellar and walk-in cheese room, but there is so much more. A slice of artisan *fromage* is the minimum you'll be leaving with. There are beautifully presented seasonal fruit and vegetables, charcuterie, temptations like house-cured gravadlax, freshly baked breads and cakes, handmade ice cream ... Mouth-watering doesn't do it justice. And if you can't wait until you get home to sample the wares, the café offers tasting plates of everything. Even better, it's licensed, so you can have a cheese-and-wine lunch to try out a few lesser-known farmhouse cheeses before you buy. And how many food shops come with two disco balls hanging from the ceiling?

2–6 Moxon Street
W1U 4EW
Tel 0207 935 0341
www.lafromagerie.co.uk

kate allden
& jane ellis

Fashionistas should head straight to KJs Laundry, a perfectly edited boutique tucked down a small laneway. Owners Kate Allden and Jane Ellis have a well-honed eye for womenswear that is stylish, individual and not what you'll see everywhere else. From quirky to classic, the selection is big on lesser-known designers, as well as some of the more mainstream names. The shop itself, with its lovely worn wooden floors and pieces of vintage furniture, is as understatedly stylish as the stock it sells. Your wardrobe will thank you.

KJs LAUNDRY
74 Marylebone Lane W1U 2PW ✤ 0207 486 7855 ✤ www.kjslaundry.com

'Londoners are very aware of style, but not afraid to be themselves'

How would you define London style?

Playful and rebellious. Londoners are very aware of style, but not afraid to be themselves, and so the result is freedom and a lack of conformity. It's the edgiest of the fashion capitals.

Where do you go in London to be inspired?

The British Museum (www.britishmuseum. org) to dip into the cultures of the world, especially their jewellery galleries. Even though the pieces are so old, they still look modern and wouldn't look out of place on today's catwalks. Very inspiring.

Your favourite local places?

The Wallace Collection (www. wallacecollection.org) for its charm—it's the perfect place to stop for tea and cake, and the rose garden at Regent's Park; so many beautiful colours and varieties.

225

What's in your secret shopping address book?

Merchant Archive in Notting Hill (www.merchantarchive.com) is a wonderful vintage shop. Just outside, Kempton Antique market (www.kemptonantiques.co.uk) is a bi-monthly market at Kempton racecourse which is great for finding new things for the house. Do a spot of haggling before rounding everything up into a van to drive home.

Where's the best place for a weekend supper?

Scotts (www.scotts-restaurant.com) in Mayfair is nice to sit at the bar, grab a quick bite and soak up the atmosphere. And the Anchor & Hope near Waterloo (www.anchorandhopepub.co.uk). It's a busy gastropub where the food is hearty and scrumptious.

Best place for a drink?

Milk and Honey (www.mlkhny.com) for the superb cocktails and quirky interior. It's like stepping into the lounge of a very rich friend with a love of the 1920s ... and it's very easy to get a bit carried away. Or The Albion in Islington (www.the-albion.co.uk) for a cosy drink—the beer garden is fab in the summer.

Your favourite breakfast spot?

Automat diner in Mayfair (www.automat-london.com) for their blueberry pancakes and Bloody Marys. It's ideally located for a stroll through Green Park, or a dip into **Dover Street Market** (see page 282) afterwards.

Where do you go in London to relax?

A walk through Kew Gardens (www.kew.org) is always a tonic, and it's so quintessentially British.

Favourite cultural sights?

The view down the river from Waterloo Bridge is a great reminder of London's history and grandeur, and the cobbled narrow streets around London Bridge evoke a feeling of old London, with sweeping views up and down the river. Also, the London Transport Museum in Covent Garden (www.ltmuseum.co.uk) is great for kids, with lots of interactive exhibits.

Top three things that every visitor to London should do?

Have fish and chips at the Golden Hind on Marylebone Lane (73 Marylebone Lane, W1U 2PN, tel 0207 486 3644); very popular and very yummy. Walk through Hyde Park, Green Park and St James's Park and just enjoy. And go to the top of Parliament Hill Fields or **Primrose Hill** (see page 36) to admire the views.

227

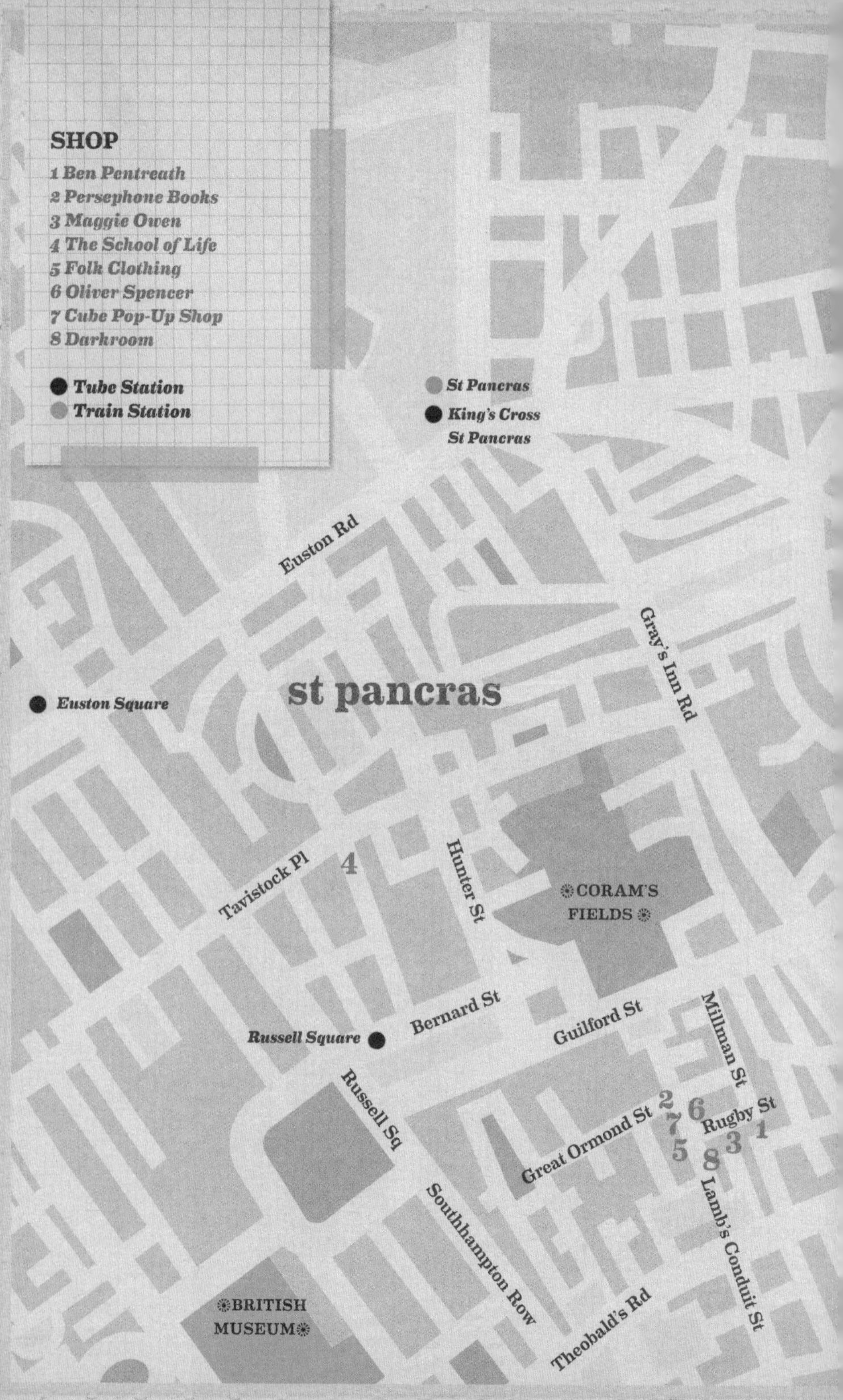
SHOP
1 Ben Pentreath
2 Persephone Books
3 Maggie Owen
4 The School of Life
5 Folk Clothing
6 Oliver Spencer
7 Cube Pop-Up Shop
8 Darkroom
Tube Station
Train Station
St Pancras
King's Cross St Pancras
Euston Rd
Gray's Inn Rd
st pancras
Euston Square
Tavistock Pl
4
Hunter St
CORAM'S FIELDS
Bernard St
Guilford St
Millman St
Russell Square
Russell Sq
Great Ormond St
2
7
6
Rugby St
3
1
5
8
Lamb's Conduit St
Southhampton Row
Theobald's Rd
BRITISH MUSEUM

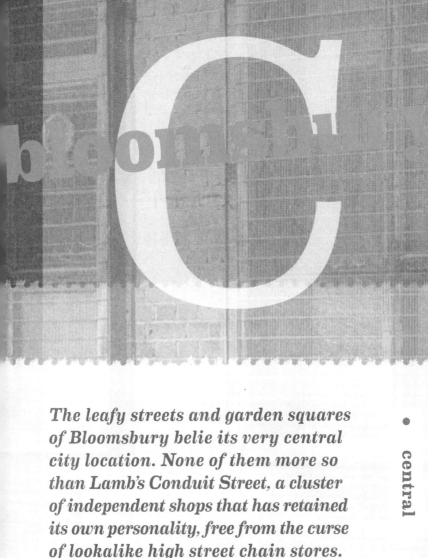

bloomsbury

*The leafy streets and garden squares
of Bloomsbury belie its very central
city location. None of them more so
than Lamb's Conduit Street, a cluster
of independent shops that has retained
its own personality, free from the curse
of lookalike high street chain stores.
A rarity. It's a lovely area for
a wander, with cultural giant the
British Museum nearby if you tire
of shopping.*

1✳ BEN PENTREATH

I defy you to leave this shop without buying something for your home. Whether it's a wooden spoon or an antique mahogany side cabinet, there is something to tempt every budget. Shelves are piled high with colourful stacks of beautiful Penguin classics and design books. On a small chair you'll find a stack of exquisitely illustrated 1940s books, among them *Elizabethan Miniatures* and *Birds of the Sea*. There's antique furniture, prints, corals and even plaster casts of Greek sculptural reliefs. If that's all too much, head for the utility side of the shop, for practical necessities such as whisks, pastry brushes, door mats and even kettle descalers. Something is sure to catch your eye.

17 Rugby Street
WC1N 3QT
Tel 0207 430 2526
www.benpentreath.com

AWAY *by* ELIZABETH ANNA HART

AWAY *by* ELIZABETH ANNA HART

AWAY *by* ELIZABETH ANNA HART

AWAY *by* ELIZABETH ANNA HART

AWAY *by* ELIZABETH ANNA HART

2*

3*

AGGIE OWE

3*

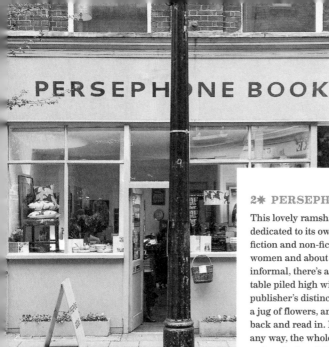

2✳ PERSEPHONE BOOKS

This lovely ramshackle bookshop is dedicated to its own imprint of neglected fiction and non-fiction 'by women, for women and about women'. Delightfully informal, there's a rickety wooden table piled high with books (all in the publisher's distinctive pale grey covers), a jug of flowers, and armchairs to settle back and read in. Not slick or styled in any way, the whole place has a charming, unique feel, and the owner's passion for literature shines through.

59 Lamb's Conduit Street
WC1N 3NB
Tel 0207 242 9292
www.persephonebooks.co.uk

3✳ MAGGIE OWEN

Surely one of the prettiest shop fronts in London, this jewellery shop is in a converted dairy, with the original frontage still intact. The pre-war building was London's first dairy, and its heritage is plain to see in the lovely old navy and white shop-front tiling and lettering. The dairy itself was a going concern until 1982. These days, the business is a well-chosen mix of contemporary jewellery and accessories, with a few quirky items such as Pakistani metal toys and patchwork fabric teddies thrown into the mix. Cast your eye across the street and there's yet more history—writers Ted Hughes and Sylvia Plath spent their wedding night at number 18.

13 Rugby Street
WC1N 3QT
0207 404 7070
www.maggieowenlondon.com

4✳ THE SCHOOL OF LIFE

This unique business could, potentially, change your life. Labelling itself 'an apothecary of ideas and mental wellness' and a 'chemist for the mind', it's both a shop and school in one. Where else can you buy books like *The Mindfulness Manifesto* or *How To Be An Agnostic* and sign up for classes on 'how to be better at internet dating', 'how to spend time alone' and 'how to balance work with life'? It's a pretty special place. The shop itself is a chic space of dark grey walls painted with the School's manifesto in bold lettering, wooden floors and unexpected touches, like a leopard-print couch and silver birch tree trunks, like sculptures growing up from the floor. Even if you leave with just a greeting card, you will feel better for having visited.

70 Marchmont Street
WC1N 1AB
0207 833 1010
www.theschooloflife.com

CLASSES SERMONS WEEKENDS

Take one of our regular evening classes and gain valuable insights into life's big issues.

Bin the Sunday papers and join the congregation at our maverick secular sermons.

Experience intellectual and social adventure on one of our weekends.

53

Folk

5✱ FOLK CLOTHING

With two shops on the same street, one menswear, one womenswear, this mini fashion empire is well worth a visit. The clothes in both outlets are a mix of own label and contemporary designers. Nothing too showy, but all of it confidently cool. The shops themselves are pared back and warehouse-like, with strip lighting hanging from coloured rope and rough concrete flooring. Look out for the sculpted marble heads in the menswear branch by British artist Paul Vanstone.

49 and 53 Lamb's Conduit Street
WC1N 3NB
Womenswear: tel 0208 616 4191
Menswear: tel 0207 404 6458
www.folkclothing.com

237

Oliver Spencer

6*

HENRI LLOYD

6✳ OLIVER SPENCER

This lovely, low-key menswear store (with a shoe shop further down the road) prides itself on its British heritage. Most of the clothes are designed and manufactured in the UK, with ninety per cent of them produced under the shop's own label. The style is traditional menswear with a casual, easy-to-wear feel. You won't find anything showy or covered in designer labels here. With its tiled fireplace, old wooden fittings and dark grey walls, the space feels more like a private home than a shop. Look out for the vintage health and hygiene posters on the wall, including one illustrating exercises for men that can be done while still enjoying a cigarette. Those were the days.
62 Lamb's Conduit Street
WC1N 3LW
Tel 0207 269 6444
www.oliverspencer.co.uk

7✳ CUBE POP-UP SHOP

There's no knowing what this shop will hold next. Thanks to the fashion PR company in the offices behind, it works as a showcase for various clients—a nautical installation of Henri Lloyd sailing gear one week, maybe work by cool young British designer Sophie Hulme the next. Pop by and take a chance.
47 Lamb's Conduit Street
WC1N 3NG
Tel 0207 242 5483
www.cubecompany.com

rhonda drakeford

If you're a fan of unusual, one-off pieces that can't be found elsewhere, then Darkroom is the shop for you. The handpicked selection of accessories for men, women and the home shines with a love of design and craftsmanship. Owners Rhonda Drakeford and Lulu Roper-Caldbeck are passionate about fusing art and design, so expect to see their own-label collections, one inspired by the 1920s Dutch De Stijl art movement, alongside indigenous African art, textiles and jewellery, and other carefully sourced pieces. Even the shop interior is a design statement, with its boldly geometric black-and-white flooring and black walls. A must-visit.

DARKROOM
52 Lamb's Conduit Street WC1N 3LL ✿ 0207 831 7244 ✿ *www.darkroomlondon.com*

'Lounge Bohemia is a brilliant little basement bar serving an unusual array of cocktails'

How would you define London style?
A mix of old and new from here and there.

Where do you go in London to be inspired?
Anywhere with oddities and strange sights, from Ridley Road food market in Dalston to The British Museum (www.britishmuseum.org).

Your favourite local places?
For the best coffee, the Espresso Room on Great Ormond Street (www.theespressoroom.com). For the best fish and chips in London, and brilliant 1960s decor, Fryers Delight (19 Theobald's Road, WC1X 8SL, tel 0207 405 4114). And for a brilliant array of fruit, veg and provisions, The People's Supermarket on Lamb's Conduit Street (www.thepeoplessupermarket.org).

Describe your perfect out-and-about weekend?
Brunch with friends, a rummage at the Hammersmith Vintage Fair (www.pa-antiques.co.uk), an old film at the British

241

Film Institute (www.bfi.org.uk) and a hearty, meaty dinner at the **Fox & Anchor** pub near Smithfield (see page 92).

What's in your secret shopping address book?

I buy trimmings and vintage ribbon at **VV Rouleaux** (see page 215), and old-fashioned and beautiful umbrellas at James Smith & Sons (www.james-smith.co.uk).

Where's the best place for a weekend supper?

A Little Of What You Fancy in Dalston (www.alittleofwhatyoufancy.info). When you get past its unassuming exterior—it's easy to miss among a row of dilapidated shops—it's a friendly, informal (and very trendy) little restaurant serving delicious and unpretentious food.

Best place for a drink?

Lounge Bohemia in Shoreditch (www.loungebohemia.com). Again, one that's easily missed—its unmarked door is sandwiched between a fast-food takeaway and a T-shirt wholesaler. It's a brilliant little basement bar serving an unusual array of cocktails from menus housed in old books. The service can be slow, but the lovely vintage furnishings are a wonderful distraction. Best to book ahead as there's no standing allowed.

Your favourite breakfast spot?

The Wolseley on Piccadilly (www.thewolseley.com). This grand establishment is housed in an old, opulently decorated car showroom and it does grand in a non-chintzy way. The breakfasts and afternoon teas make for such a nice treat, without breaking the bank.

Favourite cultural sights?

Pearly Kings and Queens in East London. You can seek them out at local fêtes and street parties, but catching sight of them by chance, like I once did (a Pearly King and Queen drove past in an old Ford Fiesta on Bethnal Green Road) is so brilliantly strange, it literally makes your day. And I love **Brixton Market** (see page 284) for the plethora of Caribbean food outlets. It's multicultural London at its noisy best.

Top three things that every visitor to London should do?

Go to the Paramount Bar (www.paramount.uk.net) on the top floor of Centre Point for a glamorous way to get one of the best bird's eye views of London. Walk around the ancient parts of the City of London at the weekend, especially Postman's Park near St Paul's Cathedral; there's a fascinating wall of Art Nouveau glazed plaques remembering acts of selflessness and bravery by ordinary people, mostly during the late 1890s. And visit Darkroom, of course!

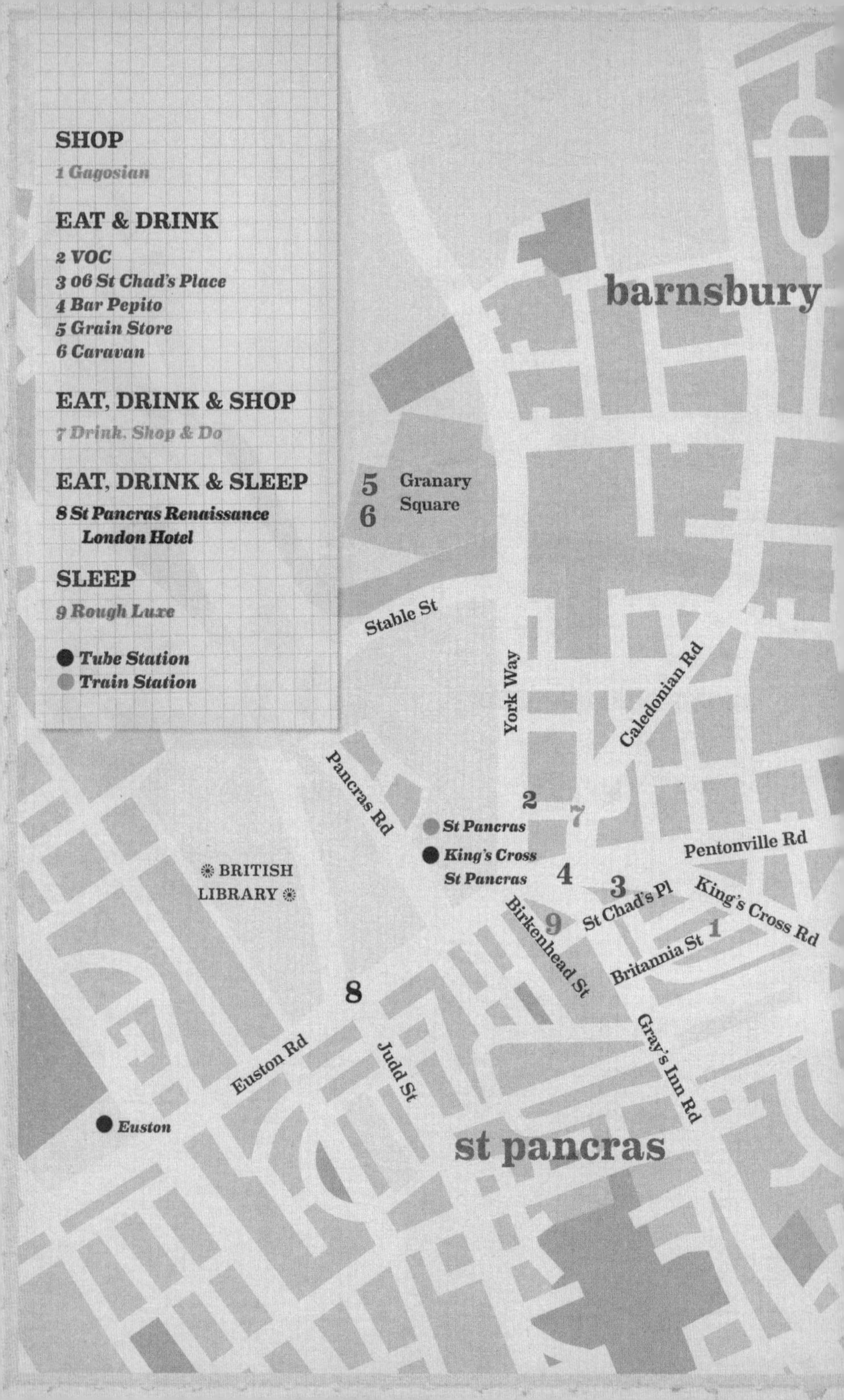

SHOP

1 Gagosian

EAT & DRINK

2 VOC
3 06 St Chad's Place
4 Bar Pepito
5 Grain Store
6 Caravan

EAT, DRINK & SHOP

7 Drink, Shop & Do

EAT, DRINK & SLEEP

8 St Pancras Renaissance London Hotel

SLEEP

9 Rough Luxe

● **Tube Station**
● **Train Station**

barnsbury

5
6 Granary Square

Stable St

York Way

Caledonian Rd

Pancras Rd

2

7

● St Pancras

● King's Cross
  St Pancras

4

3

Pentonville Rd

9 St Chad's Pl

King's Cross Rd

❀ BRITISH
LIBRARY ❀

Birkenhead St

1

Britannia St

8

Euston Rd

Judd St

Gray's Inn Rd

● Euston

st pancras

king's cross

One of London's least attractive areas has been transformed. The tangle of busy roads around King's Cross station is still grubby, but just beyond lie some urban gems. Grandest of all is the restored St Pancras Renaissance London Hotel, a Victorian Gothic masterpiece. Equally worth a visit is the regenerated Granary Square, complete with the Central Saint Martins art school campus, over 1000 choreographed fountains and two of the city's buzziest restaurants. To gaze at the architectural beauty of St Pancras, have a glass of Champagne in the hotel bar, or a delicious brunch at Granary Square, makes this once-grimy area well worth a visit.

2✳

GAGOSIAN GALLERY

1✳ GAGOSIAN

Add this to your cultural must-visit list. The gallery, part of US dealer Larry Gagosian's mega art empire, hosts some of the most interesting contemporary art shows in town. And not just 21st-century working artists—a 2010 Picasso exhibition would have had queues around the block in many cities. Here, only in-the-know Londoners trekked to King's Cross to appreciate it, and like all their other shows, entrance was free. Nondescript from the outside, the gallery opens up into two vast show spaces. Okay, so the artwork may be beyond most people's shopping budget, but the bookshop has some more affordable buys. It may be down a scruffy side street and opposite a distinctly unglamorous car park, but some of London's most exciting art world events happen here.

6–24 Britannia Street
WC1X 9JD
Tel 0207 841 9960
www.gagosian.com

2✳ VOC

Take a step back to a 17th-century drinking den at this tiny, cave-like bar. Modelled on an olde worlde punch house, it's named after the Dutch East India Company (Vereenigde Oost-Indische Compagnie), and is filled with the memorabilia of maritime travels. But the real stars are the drinks themselves. Set among the huge church candles that flicker in this sailors' den are oak barrels containing all sorts of concoctions. Rums are blended with spices such as bergamot and fresh tobacco leaf, a warm gin punch is seasoned with fresh horseradish, pressed apple and vanilla sugar. The tastes are dangerously smooth and quaffable. Tuck yourself into a shadowy corner and go exploring.

2 Varnishers Yard
Regents Quarter
N1 9AW
Tel 0207 713 8229
www.voc-london.co.uk

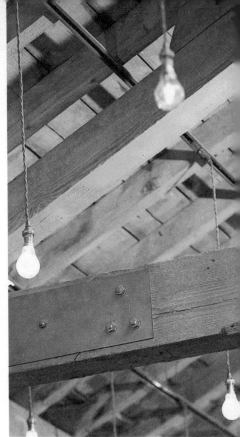

3✳ 06 ST CHAD'S PLACE

If you didn't know that this stylish bar and restaurant was at the end of this scruffy, cobbled side street, chances are you'd walk straight past. It may look unpromising, but do venture beyond the overflowing rubbish bins. The restored brick Victorian warehouse was once a mechanics workshop, long since abandoned, but is now a handsome space, with oversized wooden doors and a large skylight above the tables and Eames-style chairs. A wall-sized blown-up photograph of a train gives a nod to the area's railway heritage. If you can forgive the shabby exterior, it's a very nice place for an evening out.

6 St Chad's Place
WC1X 9HH
Tel 0207 278 3355
www.6stchadsplace.com

249

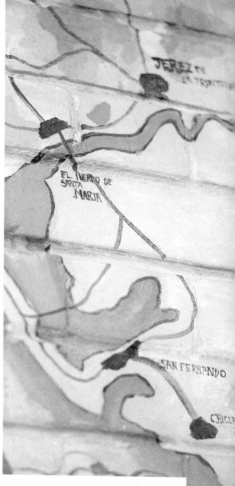

4✳ BAR PEPITO

Blink and you'll miss this tiny 'bodega' sherry bar. It's a small slice of Spain, in the middle of grimy London. With its beautifully patterned, tiled floor and tables fashioned from sherry casks, the bar is the younger sibling of the bigger Camino tapas bar across the courtyard, and it's definitely the more appealing of the two. Choose from the 15 sherries on offer, order a plate of olives, almonds and hand-carved *jamón*, and transport yourself to Andalucia.

3 Varnishers Yard
N1 9DF
Tel 0207 841 7331
www.barpepito.co.uk

BAR PEPITO

TIME OUT BAR OF THE YEAR 2010

*Sherry is superb stuff and hailed as the next big thing.
A rustic, Andalucian bodega-style bar truly dedicated to
sherry, with jaw-droppingly good tapas – terrific spot.*
Time Out

*Sherry is hip, its surging popularity enhanced by the
opening of London's first sherry bar.
The wine world's best kept secret is out.*
Decanter

*Where better to sip some of the finer offerings from
Spain than London's first sherry bar?*
The Independent

*Welcoming and unpretentious, with excellent meats and
cheeses and exquisite wine and sherry by the glass.
As authentic as it gets.*
View London

*The tiny room is a faithful replication of a jolly bodega
without the Viva España kitsch.*
Square Meal

251

5✳ GRAIN STORE

From the team behind Clerkenwell's **The Zetter Townhouse** hotel (see page 90), comes a restaurant so delicious that one visit won't be enough. Chef Bruno Loubet's kitchen serves wildly imaginative dishes that put vegetables at the heart of the menu—although it's not a vegetarian restaurant. Taste combinations such as buttermilk and carraway braised cauliflower, and smoked beetroot with pink grapefruit, are out of this world. The setting is equally creative. The large industrial space, with open kitchen, buzzes with action and detail everywhere you look—shelves of produce for the kitchen, pans hanging from meat hooks, large communal tables, as well as more intimate seat-settings. Everything is mixed up and blurred into one big, dramatic space, humming with busy chefs and very happy customers. Children are welcomed warmly, given packs of pens and paper, and encouraged to leave an artwork on the picture wall. Once a month, a junior winner scoops a free family brunch.

Granary Square
1–3 Stable Street
N1C 4AB
Tel 0207 324 4466
www.grainstore.com

6✳ CARAVAN

With the original still doing a roaring trade in Clerkenwell (see page 88), the Caravan team have expanded to a spacious warehouse-like room that is always packed. Whether it's Saint Martins professors and students popping in for takeaway cakes and savoury muffins, the weekend brunch crowd who know that Caravan serves one of London's best coffees, local workers devoted to the highly rated lunchtime pizzas, or the supper crowd sharing large platters of wagyu ribeye, roasted pollock with saffron or duck and cassoulet beans, Caravan delivers outstanding food around the clock. Together with Grain Store next door, Caravan ensures that Granary Square is one of London's newest and best foodie destinations. Those Saint Martins students don't know how lucky they are.

No 1 Granary Square
Granary Building
N1C 4AA
Tel 0207 101 7661
www.caravankingscross.co.uk

7 ✳ DRINK, SHOP & DO

This Victorian bathhouse has been transformed into a vintage and craft shop, with café, and is so unlike anything else in the area that it has to be visited to be believed. Quite what the customers of the adult bookshop next door make of the embroidery patterns and jars of old-fashioned sweets, it's hard to guess. The whole place has a jaunty, sunny feel, from the orange-and-white striped ceiling to the cheery old-fashioned tunes being played as background music. Come in here simply to shop—everything you can see, including the vintage furniture, is for sale—or sign up for a 'do' craft session, like a pin-up hair and makeup class. The café, serving lunch, afternoon tea and cocktails, is at the back, where the space unexpectedly opens up under a huge skylight which floods the space with light. Hard to think of a nicer spot for Sunday Scrabble—or one where the competitor with the highest word score gets a free cocktail. A little bit of charm amidst the King's Cross grunge.

9 Caledonian Road
N1 9DX
Tel 0207 278 4335
www.drinkshopdo.com

9✳ ROUGH LUXE

Of all the hotels you'd expect to find in this area (many insalubrious and 'pay by the hour'), a quirky design gem is not among them. Describing itself as 'half rough, half luxury', this ten-room establishment is the unique vision of designer Rabih Hage, who has transformed the Grade II listed terrace into a shabby-chic wonderland. The 'rough' element comes from walls stripped back to reveal the original plasterwork and fragments of wallpaper, and wooden floors left bare and unvarnished. For the 'luxe', striking artwork from the artists-in-residence, chandeliers, luxurious bed linen and handmade toiletries. Some rooms are tiny, but the design is so impressive that they work. And where else in the area can you breakfast in the garden, on toast and honey from the bees that live on the roof?

1 Birkenhead Street
WC1H 8BA
Tel 0207 837 5338
www.roughluxe.co.uk

255

harry handelsman

A whole book could be devoted to the restoration of the Victorian Gothic building that was originally The Midland Grand Hotel. Opened in 1873 by Queen Victoria, the building had stood derelict for years before being reborn in 2011 as the St Pancras Renaissance London Hotel. It is, quite simply, one of London's architectural masterpieces. Splash out and book a room, or just visit the beautiful Gilbert Scott bar for a glass of Champagne (less packed and much prettier than the always-busy Booking Office bar). A driving force behind the rescue of the St Pancras is property developer Harry Handelsman, for whom the building is an absolute passion. His Manhattan Loft Corporation has created luxe apartments alongside the hotel, for a lucky few who get to wake up in the midst of all the architectural splendour. There isn't a piece of rare, original wallpaper in the place that Harry doesn't know and love. London owes him a big thank you.

ST PANCRAS RENAISSANCE LONDON HOTEL
Euston Road NW1 2AR ❧ 0207 841 3540 ❧ www.stpancrasrenaissance.co.uk

> *'We are so spoilt in London as there are so many parks and open spaces'*

How would you define London style?
Laidback, cool and creative.

Where do you go in London to be inspired?
London has so many places you can go to be inspired. I love the Tate Modern (www.tate.org.uk) because they always have such wonderfully thoughtful exhibitions. I also love opera, and to be able to enjoy it in such beautiful surroundings as The Royal Opera House (www.roh.org.uk) is a real treat.

Your favourite local places?
I still love the Groucho Club (www.thegrouchoclub.com). It is so effortlessly cool, and it's close to my office so I go there a lot.

Describe your perfect out-and-about weekend?
My perfect weekend would involve cycling round Hyde Park on Boris Bikes with my daughter, having a coffee by the Serpentine and taking in an exhibition at the Royal Academy (www.royalacademy.org.uk). We are so spoilt in London as there are

257

so many parks and open spaces, so many wonderful museums and such beautiful architecture.

What's in your secret shopping address book?

Spencer Hart on Savile Row are the best tailors in London in my opinion (www.spencerhart.com). For grooming, I go to Carmelo Guastella, who owns the fantastic Melogy Men's Grooming Ltd (St Pancras Renaissance London Hotel, tel 0207 383 0027). He is utterly charming and men come from all over London to get their hair cut by him. I recently gave my daughter a bag from Bottega Veneta (www. bottegaveneta.com)—she was thrilled! And I also think Anya Hindmarch (www.anyahindmarch.com) makes the most beautiful bags.

Where's the best place for a weekend supper?

I love Pizza East on Portbello Road (www.pizzaeast.com). It is tiny, but with delicious pizzas, a great atmosphere and friendly service.

Best place for a drink?

The Fumoir Bar at Claridges (www. claridges.co.uk); it's so elegant and refined.

Your favourite breakfast sptot?

The Booking Office at the St Pancras Renaissance London Hotel—I am there for breakfast at least three times a week, so it's lucky I like it. It is the old Victorian ticket booking office and you can still see all the original features, like the ticket-booth windows. I also love to be able to look out of the window onto the St Pancras train station platform and see the Eurostar coming and going. The food is also delicious, with fantastic service; it's a great way to start the day.

Where do you go in London to relax?

Hyde Park, it is so beautiful.

Favourite cultural sights?

I like to be challenged by art, so one of my favourite galleries is White Cube in Hoxton Square (www.whitecube.com). A visit there is always enlightening. They show very high-quality work and there are always interesting people popping in and out. I also like the Albert Memorial in Hyde Park. It was designed by Sir George Gilbert Scott, who was also the architect of the St Pancras Renaissance London Hotel. I have a new-found respect for him now.

Top three things that every visitor to London should do?

Ride a Boris Bike in Hyde Park—I think these rent-by-the-hour bikes will become as much a part of London imagery as red buses and black taxis. It's a really great scheme, so easy to use and a great way to see London. Go to The Proms at the Royal Albert Hall (www.royalalberthall.com), it is such an English tradition. Obviously the last night is the most famous, but you are guaranteed a wonderful evening on any Prom night. I went three times last year. Finally, walk around. There is so much to see and do in London. It is such a wonderful, vibrant city that even just by strolling around you can feel uplifted and inspired. I have lived here for twenty years and still I can walk around and see things that I have never noticed before. It is a revelation.

259

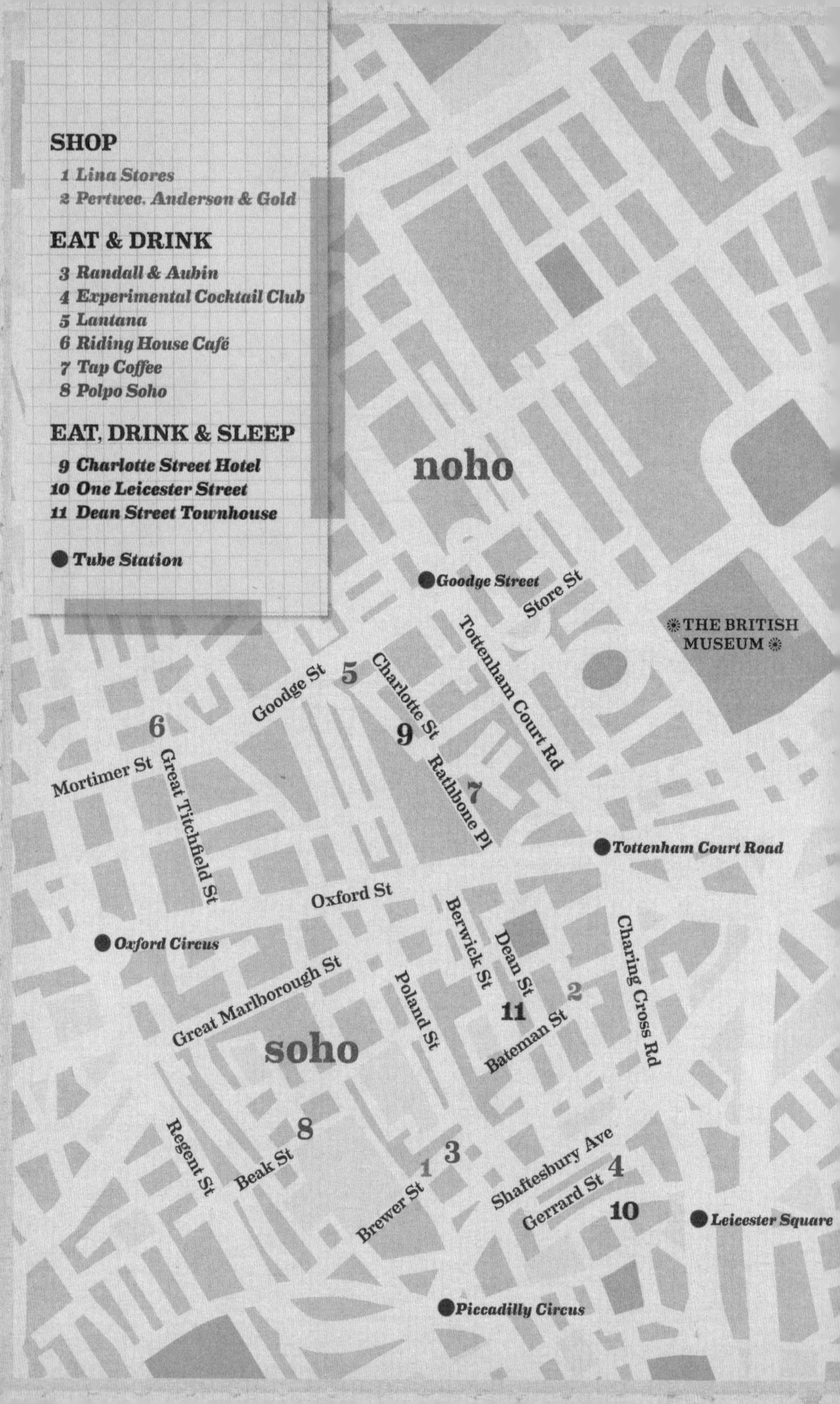
SHOP
1 Lina Stores
2 Pertwee, Anderson & Gold
EAT & DRINK
3 Randall & Aubin
4 Experimental Cocktail Club
5 Lantana
6 Riding House Café
7 Tap Coffee
8 Polpo Soho
EAT, DRINK & SLEEP
9 Charlotte Street Hotel
10 One Leicester Street
11 Dean Street Townhouse
Tube Station
noho
Goodge Street
Store St
THE BRITISH MUSEUM
Tottenham Court Rd
Goodge St
Charlotte St
Mortimer St
Great Titchfield St
Rathbone Pl
Tottenham Court Road
Oxford St
Oxford Circus
Berwick St
Dean St
Charing Cross Rd
Great Marlborough St
Poland St
Bateman St
soho
Regent St
Beak St
Brewer St
Shaftesbury Ave
Gerrard St
Leicester Square
Piccadilly Circus
1
2
3
4
5
6
7
8
9
10
11

Soho & noho

Chances are you'll be heading to Oxford Street to do some shopping at some point during your stay. Chances are you'll want to get the hell out of there as soon as possible. The big-name stores are great, the crowds are not. Head down one of the many side streets north or south, and you'll find yourself in the small streets of Soho and Noho (as the area to the north has been christened). Yes, Soho was once known for its sleaze and sex shops, but these days it's home to some of London's best bars and restaurants. Many are Michelin-starred establishments, but there has been an explosion of fantastic, great-value cafés and small restaurants, and you'd be mad to miss them. You'll need a drink after those Oxford Street hordes.

1✳ LINA STORES

This charming family-run Italian delicatessen is a Soho institution. It was given a makeover last year, but its distinctive green and white tiling and thick marble counter remain unchanged. Famous for its homemade pasta, it also sells pretty much any Italian foodstuff you can think of, from polenta, rice and biscotti, to salamis, cheeses and homemade pesto. As for olive oil, take your pick from over 15 varieties. Grab a coffee from the counter at the back, browse the shelves and buy yourself something delicious to take home.

18 Brewer Street
W1F OSH
Tel 0207 437 6482
www.linastores.co.uk

2✳ PERTWEE, ANDERSON & GOLD

In the market for some artwork? This small gallery, co-owned by actor Sean Pertwee, is the perfect place to start. In contrast to the usual architectural white-cube style of exhibition spaces, this has been reconstructed to resemble a Georgian house. With dark wooden floors and intricate white cornicing, it eschews the sterile arthouse look for the chic, elegant feel of a gentleman's club. Big spenders get to enter through a jungle-like garden at the back of the house—who knew there were palm trees in Soho?—and peruse their purchases in a cosy faux-Georgian boudoir, complete with red velvet sofas and dark parquetry floor. The rest of us might not be so lucky, but it's definitely worth popping in, even if it is through the front door.

15 Bateman Street
W1D 3AQ
Tel 0207 734 9283
www.pertweeandersongold.com

3✳ RANDALL & AUBIN

The heritage of this restaurant is clear from its lovely gold-lettered shop front. It was opened in 1911 as a butcher's by Morin Randall and Cavenur Aubin, whose names are resplendent above the door. A restaurant since 1996, it retains all the charm and history of the original establishment, but these days it does a brisk trade in Champagne and oysters rather than pork chops. And I doubt Messrs Randall and Aubin would have thought much of the chandeliers and glitter ball. Most nights, there's a queue of Soho's bright young things sipping drinks as they wait for a seat at one of the marble-top benches. But the seafood and rotisserie menu is worth the wait. A little bit of Victoriana brought lovingly up to date.

16 Brewer Street
W1F 0SQ
Tel 0207 287 4447
www.randallandaubin.com

4✱ EXPERIMENTAL COCKTAIL CLUB

It's easy to walk straight past this speakeasy-style bar in Chinatown. The shabby doorway amid the Peking duck restaurants and Chinese supermarkets of Gerrard Street gives nothing away. Nor do the scruffily carpeted stairs that you have to climb once you're inside. But persevere, because this tiny two-storey spot serves some of London's best cocktails, in a cool, shabby-chic interior. Settle yourself at one of the small, mirrored tables and toast the night with the likes of a Winnie The Pooh (rum, campari and a few extras) or a No Name Dropping (including sherry and ginseng liqueur). One tip: try to make a booking; it will make navigating the attitude of the doorman infinitely easier.

13a Gerrard Street
W1D 5PS
Tel 0207 434 3559
www.chinatownecc.com

4✱

5✱ LANTANA

Describing itself as a 'little bit of Australia' in the heart of London, this tiny café is pretty much always packed. Breakfast is especially busy—no surprise, with a menu of toasted banana bread with blossom honey and cinnamon labna, and grilled haloumi with roasted cherry tomatoes, rocket and red onion salad, poached egg and pesto on toasted sourdough. Londoners aren't used to such an antipodean blend of flavours, and they are lapping it up. Decor-wise, things are kept simple, with the space dominated by a black and white mural on the back wall, by Melbourne artist Kat Macleod. Depicting the invasive weed lantana, after which the café is named, the artwork also features other Aussie flora and fauna, to remind any visiting Australians of home.

13 Charlotte Place
W1T 1SN
Tel 0207 637 3347
www.lantanacafe.co.uk

6✱ RIDING HOUSE CAFÉ

Squirrels on the walls and some of the friendliest staff in London—what's not to love about this place? With the feel of a New York brasserie, but with delightfully quirky touches (like those squirrel wall lights), this bar and restaurant has drawn crowds from day one. Book one of the sexy booths in the main restaurant, or for a more casual meal, perch up at the bar or at the huge communal table with its nailed-down cinema seats as chairs. Food ranges from 'small plates' to share (beetroot carpaccio with sheep's ricotta, cured sea trout with jalapeño and crème fraîche), through to the ever-popular Titchfield Burger with foie gras. The private dining room, The Stables, describes itself as 'an equestrian lodge'. The mind boggles.

43–51 Great Titchfield Street
W1W 7PQ
0207 927 0840
www.ridinghousecafe.co.uk

7✱ TAP COFFEE

Coffee is a very serious business at this small side-street café. Generally regarded as one of London's best barista spots, its motto is 'making the ordinary, extraordinary'. Which means high-quality fixtures and fittings—lovely solid wooden tables and benches, nicely weighty cups and quirky vintage spoons —as well as coffee beans from artisan roasteries and a small menu of simple but delicious snacks. Local workers claim the breakfast toast is the tastiest and best-value in all London. Well worth a detour if you're shopping on Oxford Street and want to rest your weary legs.

26 Rathbone Place
W1T 1JD
www.tapcoffee.co.uk

'Generally regarded as one of
London's best barista spots,
its motto is "making the
ordinary, extraordinary"'

9*

10

9*

9

10*

10*

9* CHARLOTTE STREET HOTEL

Another of Kit Kemp's London hotels (see page 76), the 52-room Charlotte Street Hotel is a brilliantly central city base to stay, but also the perfect spot for an early evening drink. Do as the local workers do: if the weather's nice, grab a table beneath the stripy awnings on the pavement-side terrace (next to the outsized tubs of olive trees) and watch the street life go by. Cosier evenings in the bar are just as fun, with its warm tones of pink and purple velvets, and striped and kilim-patterned upholstery. The hotel also has a small private screening room, with a regular Sunday film club of dinner and a movie. A lovely way to round off the weekend.

15–17 Charlotte Street
W1T 1RJ
Tel 0207 806 2000
www.firmdale.com

10* ONE LEICESTER STREET

Its location is at the wrong end of Soho, but this discreet hotel is a gem. It may be on a pedestrianised street that separates Chinatown from the tacky chaos of Leicester Square, but once through the front door, all is elegant and calm. It's a low-key place, with just 15 rooms above the restaurant and bar, all small but sleekly designed. Squeeziest of all are the 'post-supper rooms', billed as a bed for the night when you can't face a taxi home after dinner. Whatever the size, all the bedrooms are minimally chic, supremely comfortable, and blessed with what must be the best sound-proofing in London. But the bar and restaurant are the true stars here. The bar is in the very capable hands of the Talented Mr Fox, one of London's leading cocktail teams. And boy do they take their cocktails seriously. Definitely one to seek out.

1 Leicester Street
WC2H 7BL
Tel 0203 301 8020
www.oneleicesterstreet.com

11✳ DEAN STREET TOWNHOUSE

Overnight locations don't come more in-the-thick-of-it than smack-bang in the centre of Soho. This 39-bedroom boutique hotel, spread over two Georgian townhouses, is in the heart of the action, but the hotel itself is so seductive that you might be tempted to stay put. Rooms range from Tiny (15 square metres) up to Bigger, but whatever the dimensions, they're all slick, beautifully designed and luxurious. Broom Cupboard may be little more than a crash-pad, but it's a gorgeous one, with a small ensuite that outdoes what many larger hotel rooms can offer. If you can, treat yourself to a Bigger, and enjoy a four-poster bed with a deep roll-top bath at the end of it. Very sexy. Design throughout the hotel is cosy glam, with lots of velvet upholstery, dark wood, chandeliers and flickering candles. More like a country house than a heart-of-the-city abode. The hotel's bar and restaurant is permanently crammed with Londoners. No wonder. With discerning regulars like Nigella Lawson (she has a favourite breakfast table), artwork from the likes of Tracy Emin and Peter Blake on the walls and a menu that offers traditional British dishes with a twist, it's one of the city's most grown-up and gorgeous spots.

69–71 Dean Street
W1D 3SE
Tel 0207 434 1775
www.deanstreettownhouse.com

russell norman

To open one tiny no-bookings restaurant in Soho, and have it packed from day one, is quite an achievement. To build an empire of some of London's most popular eating spots makes you a legend in restaurant circles. Russell Norman's eateries now include Polpo Soho (the original), Polpetto (run by Russell's protégée chef, Florence Knight, now a star in her own right) and the newest addition, The Ape & Bird Public House. Inspired by the scruffy bars of downtown New York, and the 'bacari' bars of Venice that serve 'cicheti' bar snacks, the restaurants share a casual, cool scruffiness and an absolute dedication to delicious food. As for Russell's next move? Watch this space.

❋ **Polpo Soho—41 Beak Street W1F 9SB** ❋ **0207 734 4479** ❋ *www.polpo.co.uk*
❋ **Polpo Covent Garden—6 Maiden Lane WC2E 7NA** ❋ **0207 836 8448**
❋ **Polpo Smithfield—3 Cowcross Street EC1M 6DR** ❋ **0207 250 0034**
❋ **Polpo Notting Hill—126–128 Notting Hill Gate W11 3QG** ❋ **0207 229 3283**
❋ **Spuntino—61 Rupert Street W1D 7PW** ❋ *www.spuntino.co.uk*
❋ **Mishkin's—25 Catherine Street WC2B 5JS** ❋ **0207 240 2078** ❋ *www.mishkins.co.uk*
❋ **Polpetto—11 Berwick Street W1F 0PL** ❋ **0207 439 8627** ❋ *www.polpetto.co.uk*
❋ **The Ape & Bird Public House—142 Shaftesbury Avenue WC2H 8HJ** ❋ **0207 836 3119**
   www.apeandbird.co.uk

'I have an admiration for Centre Point. It's like a 28-storey cheese grater'

How would you define London style?
London has such a strong sense of history
that it can't help but be partly defined by it,
so it will always be underlined by the classic
and the traditional: St Paul's Cathedral,
Tower Bridge, The National Gallery (www.
nationalgallery.org.uk), Somerset House, etc.
But I have noticed recently how distinct and
different its neighbourhoods have become.
Shoreditch, Hoxton, Dalston and Bethnal
Green are intensely vibrant right now, and it
feels like they're setting the pace for the city's
present and future. We live in exciting times.

Where do you go to be inspired?
My dog and I enjoy long walks through
Greenwich Park. The view from the
observatory is spectacular and reminds me
what a glorious city London can be. I always
get a thrill at the British Library (www.
bl.uk), particularly from the huge Eduardo
Paolozzi sculpture of *Newton, After William
Blake* in the piazza. I also have an admiration
for Centre Point (www.centrepointlondon.
com), architect Richard Seifert's glorious
1960s concrete monolith. It's like a 28-storey

cheese grater. I recommend standing in the middle of Waterloo Bridge for inspiration, too.

Your favourite local places?

Regent's Park Zoo (www.zsl.org), Blackheath, the mixed-bathing pond on Hampstead Heath, the Royal Observatory in Greenwich (www.rmg.co.uk), The Horniman Museum (www.horniman.ac.uk) in South London and Borough Market, to name a tiny few.

What's in your secret shopping address book?

The two Soho delicatessens, I Camisa (www.icamisa.co.uk) and **Lina Stores** (see page 262), both friendly Italian delis with good produce. I like The Vintage Showroom in Earlham Street (www.thevintageshowroom.com) for 1940s knitwear and accessories. Paul A. Young on Wardour Street (www.paulayoung.co.uk) stocks Mast Brothers chocolate—my gentle addiction that I'm completely in control of. **Daunt Books** in Marylebone (see page 215) is my favourite bookshop; Henry Pordes on Charing Cross Road (www.henrypordesbooks.com) is excellent for first editions and bookish gifts. There are other shops I couldn't do without, but they're hardly secret, like Liberty's menswear department (www.liberty.co.uk), which always carries an artfully curated collection of classics and slightly cutting-edge pieces.

Where do you go to relax?

If I have a couple of hours to kill I might pop into the Prince Charles Cinema (www.princecharlescinema.com). There is usually a good, slightly arty repertoire.

Where's the best place for a weekend supper?

At home with my wife and children. On rare date nights out, we like to start with a spritz at Polpo's Campari bar and then have supper in Soho, somewhere informal where the food is great. For a fancier meal, it might be Roka (www.rokarestaurant.com) in Fitzrovia, or J. Sheekey in Covent Garden (www.j-sheekey.co.uk).

Best place for a drink?

Everyone knows The Dog & Duck (18 Bateman Street, W1D 3AJ, tel 0207 494 0697) is the best pub in Soho. It pulls a great pint of Timothy Taylor's Landlord. But the best pub in London is the Jerusalem Tavern in Clerkenwell (www.stpetersbrewery.co.uk).

Your favourite breakfast spot?

Breakfast is for wimps. I'll have an espresso macchiato from Flat White on Berwick Street (www.flatwhitecafe.com). If I have a very early start and find hunger pangs interfering with my concentration, I might treat myself to a bacon sarnie on white bread from Bar Bruno (101 Wardour Street, W1F OUG, tel 0207 734 3750), one of the last greasy spoons in Soho. Or a buttery croissant and café au lait at Maison Bertaux on Greek Street (www.maisonbertaux.com).

Favourite cultural sights?

The National Theatre (www.nationaltheatre.org.uk) on the South Bank is one of my favourite destinations. It has a great bookshop, and if you like brutalist modern architecture, you'll love the building: it's a concrete masterpiece. The Donmar Warehouse (www.donmarwarehouse.com) and The Almeida (www.almeida.co.uk) have quality theatre too.

Top three things every visitor to London should do?

Take a clipper from Westminster to Greenwich (www.thamesclippers.com); London looks totally different from the water. Be photographed on the Abbey Road zebra crossing, and go to the Tate Modern (www.tate.org.uk). It really is a brilliant gallery, the building is a modern icon, and it's free.

off the map

Too good to leave out just because they don't fit into any of the book's chapters, these are a few standout favourites that deserve a mention. Of course, London is filled with many more must-see spots, and the beauty of the city is that there's always somewhere new to stumble across. These are just a few that are worth seeking out if you're in the area—no doubt you'll discover some more favourites of your own.

1✴ PETERSHAM NURSERIES

Leave the city behind and head to green and pleasant Richmond, for one of the most picturesque eating and shopping spots in London. Set in the actual working Victorian nurseries of Petersham House, the lunch-only restaurant must be one of the few eateries in London with garden-dirt flooring. Flavours are fresh and seasonal, with a short menu of simple dishes, all featuring herbs, salads, heritage vegetable varieties and fruit from the estate's garden. But it's the location that delights, as much as what is on the plate. In a word, magical. From the greenhouse setting of the restaurant itself, to the adjacent shop offering plants and small bits and pieces of homeware, not to mention the surrounding lush Thames-side water meadows, this really is an idyllic spot. Hard to believe that central London is just a few miles away.

Church Lane, off Petersham Road
Richmond
Surrey TW10 7AG
Tel 0208 940 5230
www.petershamnurseries.com

2✷ DOVER STREET MARKET

Not so much a shop as a collective of fashion installations under one roof, Mayfair's Dover Street Market is a non-negotiable destination for anyone who appreciates stylish shopping. Opened in 2004 by Rei Kawakubo of Comme des Garçons, it stocks the world's most cutting-edge labels—many of them, like Azzedine Alaia, Lanvin and Celine, with their own mini-spaces conceived as one-off experiences by the designers themselves. (The shop closes twice a year for a two-day 'Tachiagari' refit, when the likes of designers Rick Owens, Phoebe Philo and Alber Elbaz personally oversee the new configurations.) Walking in to the ground floor of concrete flooring, fantastical chandeliers and a display cabinet of skulls, it's impossible to imagine what awaits you on all six levels. And when retail fatigue kicks in, head to the delicious Rose Bakery on the fourth floor for a cup of tea and cake. A unique shopping experience.

17–18 Dover Street
W1S 4LT
Tel 0207 518 0680
www.doverstreetmarket.com

3✷ THE CROSS

London's original boho-chic bolthole in Holland Park is still going strong. Its stock of women's clothes and accessories, plus the odd bit of vintage furniture, is a kaleidoscope of colours, patterns and textures. If you're a fan of head-to-toe black, this is not the place for you. Think luxe hippy chic—these are clothes to have fun in. Even the shop decor will put you in a good mood, with its strings of bright paper lanterns, fairy lights and quirky decorative details. The building, on the corner of a street of pastel-coloured, stuccoed houses, is about as picturesque as it gets.

141 Portland Road
W11 4LR
Tel 0207 727 6760
www.thecrossshop.co.uk

3*

283

4✳

4✳ BRIXTON VILLAGE MARKET

This book's photographers Jess and Martin rate this as one of their favourite haunts in London. And certainly foodies cannot get enough of the smorgasbord of restaurants and shops in Brixton Village, the 1930s market arcade that has been rescued and revitalised in recent years. If you want to experience, under one roof, the tastes of the myriad cultures that exist in London, this is the place to come. It may not be as polished as many of the venues featured in this book, but the market's atmosphere is electric, especially on Thursday and Friday nights when it stays open late. There are too many culinary temptations for just one visit, but ones to put on your menu include Thai at family-run KaoSarn, rare-breed Yorkshire pig burgers at Honest Burgers, and exotic store cupboard buys like chilli and mango ketchup at Brixton Cornercopia.
Granville Arcade
Atlantic Road
SW9 8PS
www.honestburgers.co.uk
brixtoncornercopia.ning.com

5✳

5✳ GRANGER & CO. WESTBOURNE GROVE

Australian restaurateur Bill Granger is a star back home—and Londoners have fallen in love with his seemingly effortless café cuisine, too. With two London outposts to choose from (Notting Hill and Clerkenwell), it's the original Westbourne Grove one that draws the biggest crowds. The bright, light and airy dining room has all the beloved trademarks of his Sydney café, Bills: easy, breezy food with a decidedly Aussie feel, sleek, clean interior design and a great cup of coffee. Shame about the no-bookings policy, but this is food worth queueing for.
175 Westbourne Grove
W11 2SB
Tel 0207 229 9111
www.grangerandco.com

6✳ UPSTAIRS AT RULES

The restaurant downstairs is one of the oldest in London, founded in 1798 and famous for its traditional British dishes such as game and oysters. But it's the cocktail bar, Upstairs at Rules, that is the insider's secret—there's minimal signage. Simply ask the restaurant's doorman, and he will open a discreet side door and usher you up the stairs. At the top, you'll find a dark-wood room decorated with hunting scene murals, old-fashioned tassled light fittings and patterned carpets. With its red leather chairs and red velvet booths, it has the feel of a gentleman's club, all very horse and hounds. It's a quiet, undiscovered spot, perfect for avoiding the Covent Garden crowds and enjoying a grown-up cocktail or two.

35 Maiden Lane
Covent Garden
WC2E 7LB
Tel 0207 836 5314
www.rules.co.uk

OLYMPIC STUDIOS

7*

Savouries

Goat's cheese &
caramelized onion tart·
5
Pork & sage sausage roll·5
Classic Quiche·5
Chanterelle & Cheddar
Tart·6

7*

8*

8*

LASSCO

7✳ OLYMPIC STUDIOS

It took four years, but determined Barnes locals Lisa and Stephen Burdge have transformed an abandoned piece of history into a community jewel. Built in 1906 as a dance hall and theatre, Olympic Studios became, in the 1960s, one of London's starriest recording studios. The Rolling Stones, Jimi Hendrix, The Beatles, David Bowie and Queen all worked here ... and then, in 2009, it closed. Horrified by developers' plans for a supermarket and apartments, the Burdges came to the rescue, creating one of the buzziest venues south of the river. Entertainment is still at its heart, with two state-of-the-art cinemas, and a downstairs cafe and dining room. But the real treat is the Members' Club bar and restaurant upstairs. Find a signed-up local to get you in, then bask in the glow of a show-stopping chandelier that dominates the lofty room. Decor is vintage luxe, including fittings from a decommissioned ocean liner. The effect will take your breath away.

117–123 Church Road
London SW13 9HL
Tel 0208 912 5161
www.olympiccinema.co.uk

8✳ LASSCO BRUNSWICK HOUSE

You don't expect to find a Georgian house stuffed with treasures on one of London's bleakest roundabouts, but LASSCO is an unusual kind of place. The heritage-listed mansion is hemmed in by the busy roads of Vauxhall, but once through the grand porch entrance, all of that fades away. Suddenly, you're in the midst of architectural reclamation curiosities, all randomly displayed throughout the grand rooms of this magnificent 18th-century home. Suits of armour, huge gilt mirrors, giant chimneypieces, chandeliers and rare botanical prints—everything you see is for sale. A little piece of history definitely worth visiting, if you can forgive its rather shabby location.

30 Wandsworth Road
SW8 2LG
Tel 0207 394 2100
www.lassco.co.uk

barny read

When a blackboard sign outside a shop has an arrow and the handwritten message 'Good Shop', you'd be mad to walk past. Inside the Peanut Vendor's small space in North London's Newington Green, you'll find vintage design heaven, with a range of well-priced mid-century furniture and oddities. Owner Barny Read has a self-confessed obsession with anything old, be it records, clothes or furniture. And, along with co-owner Becky Nolan, he's turned it into his business. You might spot an industrial trolley, a stack of old school chairs or even a stuffed pigeon. This is a beautifully edited selection of quirky and cool buys, not a bit of junk in sight. Barny is passionate about finding great pieces and selling them at affordable prices—many other places would be charging a lot more—and a love of the merchandise shines through.

THE PEANUT VENDOR
133 Newington Green Road N1 4RA ❋ **0207 226 5727** ❋ **www.thepeanutvendor.co.uk**

'I love all the old buildings, there are hidden gems all over the city'

How would you define London style?

I think a lot of people my age like to buy into heritage brands. I guess it's the safety of knowing something is done well. Having said that, a lot of younger Londoners make their look work by styling charity-shop and vintage finds well.

Where do you go in London to be inspired?

Everywhere I've lived in London I'd go for a wander and be inspired. I love all the old buildings, there are hidden gems all over the city.

Your favourite local places?

Newington Green Fruit And Vegetables (109 Newington Green Rd, N1 4QY, tel 0207 354 0990) is definitely the best fruit-and-veg shop in London. Belle Epoque (www.belleepoque.co.uk) is an amazing French patisserie on Newington Green—the crumbles are another level, but nothing in there ever disappoints.

Describe your perfect out-and-about weekend?

A trip to a farmers' market to pick up some good meats, a bike ride somewhere, preferably near a good coffee, and then a wander round looking in some record shops. In an ideal world, I'd end up at Plastic People, a club in Shoreditch (www.plasticpeople.co.uk) watching Dixon play. Cab home and then breakfast at local café Acoustic (60 Newington Green, N16 9PX, tel 0207 288 1235).

What's in your secret shopping address book?

Opposite our flat is probably my favourite shop in London. It's called Sargent & Co (www.sargentandco.com) and sells bespoke bikes. It's exactly what a bike shop should be, an organised mess full of beautiful vintage frames. The smell of bike oil hits you the minute you walk through the door and every time I go past I want a new bike. Rob, the owner, hand-picks them and fixes them up to order.

Where's the best place for a weekend supper?

Trullo in Islington (www.trullorestaurant.com). It's just round the corner from the shop, off Highbury Corner. Really great Italian food and beautifully done out, a real treat.

Best place for a drink?

The Island Queen in Islington (www.theislandqueenislington.co.uk) is always nice. It's close to the canal, so you can cycle along that to get there. It's a little bit tucked away, so never too busy. And The Charles Lamb (www.thecharleslambpub.com) round the corner is good for food.

Your favourite breakfast spot?

Acoustic in Newington Green, for three reasons. One, I love the owner. Two, it's about ten metres from the shop and three, the food is always tasty and very reasonably priced.

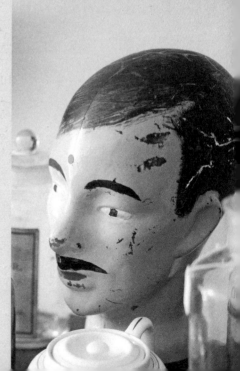

about the author

Saska Graville has worked as a writer and editor in women's magazines and newspapers for over twenty years, both in London and Sydney. She was the editor of New Woman magazine, Australia, and the features editor of The Sun-Herald newspaper in Sydney, before moving back to London as deputy editor of bestselling glossy magazine Red. She remains a UK travel correspondent for The Sun-Herald, and loves nothing more than a new hotel to review.

A BIG THANK YOU

This book could not have happened without the help of four people. First, the dynamic husband-and-wife photographic team of Jess Reftel Evans and Martin Reftel (www.amorfo.co.uk). Their energy and enthusiasm is infectious. Second, my co-researcher Alison Bakunowich, who paced the streets of London alongside me most weekends and made the whole project infinitely more fun. And lastly, art director and stylist Mary Norden, who helped to brainstorm the book idea in the first place. Thanks to Sam Baker, former editor-in-chief of Red magazine, picture director Beverley Croucher and Red's current editor-in-chief Sarah Bailey for all their help and support, to Marisa Bate and Natasha Lunn for their additional research, my agent Lizzy Kremer at David Higham Associates, and to the team at Murdoch Books—my publishers Tracy Lines and Diana Hill, project editor Sophia Oravecz and designer Miriam Steenhauer—who have all been a pleasure to work with. And a thank you to all the Londoners I encountered along the way. You're an inspiring lot and we live in a brilliant city. We should all be very proud.

First published in 2012 by Murdoch Books, an imprint of Allen & Unwin
This edition published in 2015

Murdoch Books Australia
83 Alexander Street
Crows Nest NSW 2065
Phone: +61 (0) 2 8425 0100
Fax: +61 (0) 2 9906 2218
www.murdochbooks.com.au
info@murdochbooks.com.au

Murdoch Books UK
Erico House, 6th Floor
93–99 Upper Richmond Road
Putney, London SW15 2TG
Phone: +44 (0) 20 8785 5995
www.murdochbooks.co.uk
info@murdochbooks.co.uk

For Corporate Orders & Custom Publishing contact Noel Hammond,
National Business Development Manager Murdoch Books Australia

Publisher: Diana Hill
Design concept: Tracy Lines
Design Manager: Hugh Ford
Designers: Miriam Steenhauer and Avril Makula
Cover design: Hugh Ford and Madeleine Kane
Photographers: Jessica Reftel Evans and Martin Reftel
Project editors: Sophia Oravecz and Katri Hilden
Production: Mary Bjelobrk
Maps: Netmaps®

A cataloguing-in-publication entry is available from the catalogue of the
National Library of Australia at www.nla.gov.au.

ISBN 978 1 74336 331 7 Australia
ISBN 978 1 74336 332 4 UK

A catalogue record for this book is available from the British Library.

Colour reproduction by Splitting Image Colour Studio Pty Ltd, Clayton, Victoria
Printed by 1010 Printing International Limited, China

All details referred to in this book were correct at the time of printing.
Please contact the venues directly as the details are subject to change.